John Thelwall

The Rights of Nature - Against the Usurpations of

Establishments

a series of letters to the people of Great Britain, on the state of public

affairs, and the recent effusions of the Right Honourable Edmund Burke.

First Letter

John Thelwall

The Rights of Nature - Against the Usurpations of Establishments
a series of letters to the people of Great Britain, on the state of public affairs, and the recent effusions of the Right Honourable Edmund Burke. First Letter

ISBN/EAN: 9783337195632

Printed in Europe, USA, Canada, Australia, Japan

Cover: Foto ©ninafisch / pixelio.de

More available books at **www.hansebooks.com**

THE

RIGHTS OF NATURE,

AGAINST THE

USURPATIONS OF ESTABLISHMENTS.

[PRICE TWO SHILLINGS.]

THE

RIGHTS OF NATURE,

AGAINST THE

USURPATIONS OF ESTABLISHMENTS.

A SERIES OF LETTERS TO

THE PEOPLE OF BRITAIN,

ON

THE STATE OF PUBLIC AFFAIRS,

AND

THE RECENT EFFUSIONS

OF

THE RIGHT HONOURABLE EDMUND BURKE.

———

BY JOHN THELWALL.

———

LETTER THE FIRST.

———

LONDON:

PUBLISHED BY H. D. SYMONDS, NO. 20, PATERNOSTER-ROW;
AND J. MARCH, NORWICH.

———

1796.

LETTER I.

INTRODUCTORY REMARKS; ON THE SPIRIT AND TEMPER OF BURKE'S LETTERS ON THE PROSPECT OF A REGICIDE PEACE.

THE *tocfin* of ariſtocracy ſounds once more— the *generale* is beaten on the tortured hide of " old John Ziſca," and the yell of perſecution rings through the haraſſed country. Rouſe from the couch of lethargy, O ſluggiſh and infenſate people! ſhake off the drowſy ſtupor, which, creeping over the frozen nerve of miſery, at once foothes, and threatens with the fleep of death. If neither the blood of friends nor relatives, " poured " out like water" in this profligate cruſade of the powerful and the wealthy, againſt the poor and weak—of governments, and government contractors, againſt their oppreſſed and plundered people *—If neither the ſacrifice of thouſands and tens of thouſands by the yellow peſtilence, that high prieſtefs to the Moloc of Weſt Indian ava-

* " It is in its ſpirit, and for its objeſt, a *civil war.*"—Letters, Rivington's edit. p. 144.

B   rice,

rice, who immolates the flower of Britifh youth, for the perpetuity of the African flave trade—If neither the woes, nor the infults you have endured, nor the perfecutions which have outraged all humanity, and made law a mockery; if neither the burthens under which you groan, nor the organized fyftem of monopoly (which thofe burthens have of neceffity produced) and which, worfe than a blighting mildew, hangs on the full ear of your vain profperity, counteracts the bounties of nature *, and, in fpite of an abundant harveft, denies to the craving family of the artificer and the peafant, even the *negative blefling* † of a plenteous meal—If neither of thefe, nor all accumulated together in one horrid mafs, can goad and urge you to the manly energies of reafon, and the decided tone of *authoritative* complaint—If neither the invocations nor the fufferings of the intrepid few, who, even in thefe bad times, dare to be the advocates of human rights, can warm you to fympathy, or roufe you to refleftion, yet, liften awhile to the prophetic fury of the arch-enemy of your rights and freedom : perufe the portentous leaves he has thus wildly fcattered, and think

* Bread 9d. a quartern loaf, immediately after a moft abundant harveft: The caufe of this evil, and the nature of the remedy, will be difcuffed in the following letters.

† I fhall fhew hereafter, that, in the prefent ftate of fociety, the labourer has a right to fomething more than meat, drink, fleep, and clothing, in return for his productive toil.

upon

upon the fetters that are ftill forging for you : At-
tend, I fay, to the threats fo liberally diftributed,
ftamped as it were, with the currency of authority, from the very mint of court confidence, and
iffued by the penfioned hand of an hireling apoftate, paid by the produce of *your labour* to encreafe your burthens, and deftroy your rights: and,
when you have heard thefe denunciations, which
in daring profligacy outftrip conception, and almoft
make us heretics againft our fenfes, then fink
down again, if ye can, into your wonted fupinenefs, till the " falutary, but critical terrors of the
cautery and the knife *"—the relumined fires of
Smithfield, and the axe upon Tower Hill, fhall
awaken, and warn ye that your hour is come.

For myfelf, my heart bleeds, when I think
of the abject condition to which the fpirit of
my devoted country is beaten down, when hireling plunderers, riotous paupers, dependant
upon the purfe of extorted charity (to fupport
whofe wafteful luxury the labourer muft fweat,
fo much the more at his hard drudgery, and
return at night to fo much the worfe hammock and the worfe meal) can dare to give
public utterance to fuch fentiments as thefe pamphlets contain : Sentiments which outrage all hu-

---

* Letters, p. 20. The whole paffage from which this fentence is quoted, is an after-thought. It is not to be found in
Owen's edit.

manity

manity—which defy all fhame—which breathe
the moft unqualified tyranny—excite to the moft
fanguinary perfecutions—tear afunder, with the
utmoft violence, all communion and fympathy
between the governing few and the governed
multitude *—declare open, inveterate, irrecon-
cileable war, on the part of the former, not only
againft the lives, properties, and liberties, but
againft the opinions, feelings, inclinations of the
latter—uphold the horrible doctrine of extermi-
nating opinions, and enforcing creeds and ceremonies by the fword†—threaten, with fomething more than diftant hints, the abrogation of
every provifion that ftands between the life of
the patriot, and the vengeance of a corrupt and
irritated court‡, and denounce at once, a com-

---

* It has been the fafhion, in certain affemblies, to rail
againft the practice of feparating the government from the
nation, as a new-fangled Jacobinical artifice ; and Mr. B. is moft
outrageous againft the French Directory on this account : Yet
he himfelf out-jacobinizes Jacobinifm in this way. There is,
however, nothing new in it. The diftinction is as old as hiftory,
as every man of reading well knows. The moft revered and
philofophical of the ancient hiftorians teach us by their fentiments, as well as their facts, that when governments fet up
an intereft oppofite to that of the people—the people are neceffitated to feek an intereft in oppofition to their governments.

† Thoughts, p. 63 to 68.—Owen's edit. Not in Rivington's.

‡ Letters, p. 20. If I underftand this paffage, it is a prelude
to the invafion of trial by jury. See further, p. 53, 54, &c.

puted

puted number of eighty thoufand people *, (according to the author's own account, the ftem
and flower of Britifh intellect†) to the prompt
and deftroying fury of " a vigour beyond the
law."

Yes, my heart bleeds to think that fuch men
dare to utter fuch fentiments—for though I wifh
not to ftop the current of difcuffion, either by
legal perfecution, or the fury of a mob, yet moft
certainly I do wifh to uphold the falutary awe of
popular opinion ; and, notwithftanding fome doctrines of fuppofed treafons, propagated in the late
never to be forgotten parliament, and retailed
again (if retail it could be called) in the nine
hour harangues of Adair, Scott, and Mitford, I
fhall venture to affirm, that in whatever country
this falutary awe does not operate, not only upon the tools and dependants of government, but
upon the government itfelf, *even to its higheft head*,
there tyranny, in its effence, is already eftablifhed,
and liberty is but a name.

And, how is this falutary awe to be enforced?
By the manly energies of the people—by their active vigilance, in watching the conduct of their governors, and comparing it with the fentiments of
their advocates and known retainers—by that in-

* Letters. Compare p. 19 to 22, with p. 67, 68, and 71.
† Ibid. p. 70 and 144.

tellectual

tellectual courage, which dares to give utterance to whatever the heart feels; and, above all, by that sturdy, restless, jealous exertion of the inalienable prerogative of reason, which contends, inch by inch, for the great charters of birth-right and nature, and instead of shrinking, with panic terror, at every triumph of *legal* innovation, is roused to fresh exertions by every retrenchment, and exercises, with greater ardour, the rights which yet remain. These are the means by which a brave and enlightened people *overawe* their governors, and compel them to exercise a wary and modest caution, salutary to the nation at large, and ultimately beneficial to themselves. These are the true and genuine checks of a free government. Without these, I repeat it, no government can be free. Different shapes and modes of political institution, may give to these checks a different mode of operation—a better or a worse—a more permanent, or a more precarious organization; but the principle is in the heart of the people : and where this principle is active, monarchy * itself may be attempered with a degree of liberty;

---

* By monarchy, the reader is to remember, that I mean something very different from kingly power. The former means a government *by one man*, who holds his power by some supposed or assumed *individual* right: the latter is a delegated trust, conferred by, and held for the acknowledged *benefit of the people*. Where monarchy begins, kingship ends; and the people who bargained for a king, are not bound to submit to a monarch.

without

without it, republics are but defpotifms in maf-querade.

How ftands it in this country with refpect to this falutary check, grounded (as in the enfuing letters I fhall prove it to be) in the effential rights of nature, and the very principles of political affociation? Does the government—does the le-giflature—do the minifters, or even the hireling fcribblers of thofe minifters, feel and acknowledge this controlling awe? No. The legiflature (the *late* legiflature) has ventured to call this over-awing influence of popular opinion high treafon; the minifters have declared, in exprefs terms, that they lay taxes on our fhoulders for the fupport of an immenfe troop of cavalry, to out-awe this awe, to deftroy this check, to fupprefs this opinion, to ram it down our throats with the broad fword, or drown it with the murderous roar of mufquetry; while grey-headed, penfioned apoftates—the pur-chafed panders of official corruption, bewail the pretended " relaxation of all authority *," and call aloud for laws of more fanguinary prompti-tude, and meafures of more coercive violence †, becaufe, " the crown," forfooth, cannot deftroy,

---

* Letters, p. 19.

† " The fteadinefs of the phyfician is overpowered—The doctor of the conftitution fhrinks from his own operation," &c. p. 20. The whole paffage is quoted and examined, p. 57 of this letter.

at will, whomfoever it choofes to arraign, **but**
" retires from *its courts*, defeated and difgraced *"
by the groundlefs profecutions with which its minifters infult the juftice and the feelings of the nation. Could thefe things be—could we be thus dra-
gooned and trampled upon—half gagged, and half
bullied into filence, if we were the men we have
been ?—if we inherited the fpirit of thofe anceftors, over whofe honourable graves we ftalk, an
abject and degraded progeny? No, the evil is
here. A greedy and unfocial felfifhnefs abforbs
our faculties. A bafe timidity bows our foliciting
necks to the yoke : and a want of all kindnefs,
all good faith, and all common juftice, to thofe
who embark fairly in the common caufe, palfies
every effort of patriotifm; and leaves the ifolated
wretch, whofe defperate honefty ftill prompts him
to contend with powerful ufurpation, more a'
prey to the malignant envy of thofe he endeavours
to ferve, than the perfecuting violence of the clan'
whofe corruption he has the hardihood to expofe.
Thefe difpofitions have had more to do in prof-
trating the hopes and liberties of the people, at
the footftool of borough-mongering ufurpation,
than all the proclamations and perfecutions of
the laft five years, backed and fupported with
new-fangled laws of treafon and fedition, the

* Letters, p. 20.

formidable

formidable legions of military affociators, and all the troops of fencible and yeomanry cavalry which inflate with fuch audacious confidence *the* MARAT *of the Britifh cabinet.*

While thefe difpofitions remain, the caufe of liberty will be retrogade, the beggary and wretchednefs of the multitude will continually encreafe, and the growing infolence of authorifed plunder will exult in apparent omnipotence. In fhort, while each man continues to care for no one but himfelf, all will be trampled and oppreffed ; and while the friends of liberty, unaffociated, and unendeared to each other*, inftead of confidering themfelves as one common family, cherifh their private jealoufies, and forget their common interefts, fo long will frefh projeĉts of ufurpation be formed and executed with impunity, and mankind be treated like a herd of cattle. But when the people, recovered from their panic, and roufed from their infenfibility, fhall be perfuaded to compare their faculties with their condition—

---

* It is really lamentable to recolleĉt how large a portion of thofe who have been perfecuted for their attachment to the public caufe, have either been driven to America for bread, or are pining for want of it at home. Ariftocrats will not employ the men whom they have injured, and democrats negleĉt the veterans who have ferved them. Every patriot, thus abandoned to ruin, is a feather plucked from the wing of Freedom.

C the

the fituation in which they are—and that in
which they have a right to be—when no longer
the dupes of their own miftaken felfifhnefs, they
fhall feel and acknowledge the importance of a
perfevering fortitude, and (yielding to that ftrong
fenfe of general neceffity, which annihilates, or at
leaft fufpends, the petty fa&ions of jealoufy and
envy) with a generous confidence and unanimity
fhall refolve to demand their rights; then fhall
the golden vifions of corruption fade away, and
the dark mifts of hovering defpotifm flee before
the rifing fun of Britifh freedom. Then fhall the
hireling Burke, with the whole clan of penfioned
fcribblers, inftead of yelping thus audacioufly for
the blood of their fellow citizens, bow, with be-
coming awe, to the tribunal of popular opinion,
and learn to refpe& the rights and the feelings,
not only of " four hundred thoufand political ci-
" tizens *," but of feven millions of enlightened
Britons, all confcious of their natural and civil
equality; all afferting their equal fhare in the
common inheritance of *rights*, and producing " (in
" their perfons) their title deeds†."

In the meantime, let us hope that this new outrage upon the rights, and feelings, and fecurity

---

* Letters, p. 67.
† *Paine's Firft Principles of Government.*—Intrinfically the
moft valuable of all his productions.

of mankind, will not be without its influence in
producing the defired effect: for, if ever wholefale denunciations could infpire a fenfe of common danger—and, if ever a fenfe of common
danger had the power of knitting men together
in the firm links of unanimity and common intereft, furely thefe pamphlets contain fufficient
warning, that we muft be no longer fupine, felfifh,
and divided—unlefs, indeed, we mean to be reduced to the dreadful alternative of either aban-
doning, for ever, all difcuffion of our rights—all
hope of improving our miferable condition—all
oppofition to the meafures of government, however
corrupt and tyrannical they may become, or of
refigning to profcription, legalized maffacre, or
hired affaffination, an acknowledged fifth—perhaps a third—perhaps more than half of the well
informed, reflecting, reafoning, and, what is arif-
tocratically called, *refpectable* part of the community.

This, I fay, is the plain alternative, laid down
by Mr. Burke. But I fhall not, according to his
fafhion, fatisfy myfelf with affertion. I fhall proceed to proof.

Mr. B. I fhould premife, is a very defultory,
and excentric writer. His combuftible imagination fumes, and boils, and burfts away, like
the lava from a volcano (as bright, and as

C 2   deftructive)

deftru&ive) in a thoufand different directions ; ap-
parently without art or defign. Order and ar-
rangement appear to be entirely defpifed ; pro-
portion of parts is exprefsly laid down, in his
only elementary work*, to be no ingredient of
the beautiful ; and his political publications may
be regarded as illuftrations of this curious doctrine. Tropes, fentiments, and propofitions, are
every now and then ftarting up, one knows not
why, or whence, or wherefore.

    " The things, 'tis true, are coftly, rich, and rare :
    " But wonder how the devil they got there !"

Every metaphor becomes an allegory ; every
embellifhment a digreffion ; and every digreffion
a voluminous epifode. But the reader, who, on
this account, fhould calculate upon the artleffnefs
of Mr. Burke's mind, would do no credit to his own
penetration. " If this be madnefs, there is me-
" thod in't." In this excurfive frenzy of compo-
fition, there is much deep defign and infidious
policy. He not only writes with a two-fold object—but his objects are in diametrical oppofition to each other. It is his intention at once to
inftruct and to confufe. Even in that fmall pro-
portion of the people of Britain whom he calls

  * Treatife on the Sublime and Beautiful, part III. fect.
2, 3, 4, and 5.

                                                " the

" the Britifh public," there is a ftill fmaller fub-
divifion (men of complete leifure, and of trained
political education) whom he regards as the
initiated few, and who, of courfe, may be expected to catch up, and put together, many of the
loofe disjointed hints, fcattered here and there,
with fuch ftudied careleffnefs as to efcape the
obfervation of thofe who " read as they run."
Hence, if we want to know the whole meaning,
and real object of this mafter of political contro-
verfy, inftead of following him through the regular fucceffion of pages and paragraphs, we muft
feek for the leading traits and pofitions of his
work, and then, putting together the disjointed
parts of the fyllogifm fo artfully divided, we
muft extract the enveloped conclufion for our-
felves.

Having furnifhed the reader with this clue, let
him turn to the *Letters,*" *p.* 66 *to* 71, or the
" *Thoughts,*" *p.* 16 *to* 21, then to the " *Thoughts,*"
p. 63 *to* 68, and to the " *Letters, p.* 19 *to* 23, and
he will find the dilemma I have ftated to be very
fully unfolded : that is to fay, he will find the
penfioner of an adminiftration, which has been
in the conftant practice of preparing the minds
of a certain clafs, by means of the pamphlets
and paragraphs of their hirelings, for the promul-
gation of every pre-concerted fcheme of tyranny
and

and ufurpation—he will find this penfioned pan-
der—this grey-headed procurator of profcription
and blood, ferioufly recommending, by the " fe-
" vere" and " unfhrinking operation" of fome
new means of perfecution and " *force*," the utter
extermination of every fentiment of reform—or,
as he very accurately, though infidioufly, calls it,
change *.

In the firft of thofe paffages above referred to,
Mr. B. after obferving that, " it cannot be con-
" cealed, we are a divided people," proceeds " to
" compute, and to clafs thofe, who, *in any politi-*
" *cal view*, are to be *called* the people."—" In
" England and Scotland," fays he," I compute that
" thofe of adult age, not declining in life, of *to-*
" *lerable leifure* for fuch difcuffions, and of *fome*
" *means of information*, more or lefs, and who are
" *above menial dependence*, (or what is virtually
" fuch) may amount to about *four hundred thou-*
" *fand:*" (*Letters* †, *p*. 66) to which, in his original *Thoughts* ‡, he had added—" In this num-
" ber *I include the women* who take a concern in
" thefe tranfactions, who cannot exceed twenty
" thoufand." And thus did this *preux chevalier*,
though fo furious an antagonift of the *Rights
of Man*, in an unguarded, perhaps a *tender* hour,

---

* See p. 44 of this Letter.   † Rivington's edit.
‡ Owen's edit. p. 17.

confefs

confefs himfelf a profelyte to the *rights of woman*. And this, fays he—this petty fraction of the po- pulation of England and Scotland—thefe four hundred thoufand males and females, who alone, of all the three or four millions of adults, by whom this ifland is peopled, have leifure for difcuffion, or the means of any degree of infor- mation—" *This is the Britifh public !*"—this is the " *natural* reprefentative of the people !"

O infulted and degraded Nature !—O awful aggregate of exiftence ! how is thy venerable name blafphemed, by thefe pious, canting, jugg- ling politicians ! By what right, by what omnipo- tent power, by what uncreating, and re-creating authority, does this bafe renegade doom to politi- cal annihilation nine-tenths of the adult inhabitants of a nation? Where are the fate-commanding locks of this painted Jupiter, that thus he thinks to *nod* away the exiftence of millions?—Where are his thunder-bolts and his lightnings?—But I had forgot: the lightnings and the thunderbolts are all prepared. Windham (the armed progeny of his prolific brain) keeps the key of the dread arfenal ; and if he does but turn the maffy lock, the thunders roar, the conflagration fpreads, the heavy clouds bear death and defolation on their wings, and the million trembles and obeys. But waving thefe thundering arguments (and I truft

that

that the time is not diftant when the conduĉtors
of reafon will difarm them of their terrors, and
the tempefts of minifterial fury rage innoxious !)
upon what foundation do thefe calculators take
a tenth for the whole, and call four hundred thoufand (men and *women*) " the public of Britain?"
Why, truly—the reafon is even more profligate
than the affertion itfelf!—becaufe of our whole
population not more than a tenth-part have
either the *leifure*, or the means for any degree of
" information, more or lefs !" And is this your
boafted ftate of civilization and refinement ?—Is
this the wealth, grandeur, profperity, and flou-
rifhing condition of the country ?—Is this good
order ?—Is this *government* (or is it grinding and
murderous oppreffion) which dooms the mafs of
mankind to inceffant toil, and comfortlefs affiduity,
and affigns the leifure, and the means of any degree of information or difcuffion, to a tenth-part
only of the inhabitants ? And, even of this tenth,
how large a portion are to be ranked, not
among the *promoters*, but the *deftroyers* of the
profperity fo much vaunted :—not among the.
produĉtive labourers, but among the caterpillars
and locufts, the blights and mildews of focial
induftry !—the placemen and the penfioners ; the
Burkes and the Reevefes—unprincipled fophifts hired with prodigal portions of the general
plunder,

plunder, to abufe, calumniate, and deftroy the poor wretches whom this plunder reduces to ftarving beggary.

Are thefe the inftitutions which Mr. B. wifhes to fupport? Are thefe the perfect models of focial jurifprudence which it is blafphemy to approach with the unhallowed finger of innovation or reform? Are thefe (in their effects) the regular and orderly fabrics of the ancient legitimate " government of ftates," whofe plans and materials were " drawn from the old Germanic " or Gothic cuftumary *," and of which thofe famous architects, " the civilians, the jurifts, and " the publicifts," have given us fuch flattering draughts, ground plots and elevations? If they are, perifh, I fay, fuch temples of oppreffion and injuftice! Away with your idle jargon of *venerable* antiquity :—that awful, but endearing epithet, belongs not, Mr. *Burke*, to grey hairs alone. Away with your pompous boafts of grace, beauty, and fublimity, of fwelling proportions, and polifhed fymmetry. If fuch are the effects of thefe fabrics, they are hateful and accurfed ; and, though crowned with " Corinthian capitals," though hung with antique trophies of renown, and adorned with offerings of ancient and modern piety, they muft perifh ; they ought to perifh ; and they

* Letters, p. 110. Thoughts, p. 49.

D   will.

will. They are Augean ftables that muft be cleanfed. They are Baftilles of intelleЄt, which muft be deftroyed. They are infulting maufoleums of buried rights, and are ready to totter from their bafe ; for the day of the refurrection is near at hand; and " the vail of the temple fhall " be rent in twain.."

But no, Mr. B. you are a flanderer of the inftitutions you pretend to fupport. Things are not yet fo bad as you reprefent them ; though if you and your confederates were fuffered to proceed in your infamous career, there is no knowing how foon we might fink even to a ftill lower ftate of degradation. The number of thofe, who, fome how or other, find, or *make*, the means and opportunities of obtaining *fome degree* of information, is not yet reduced to one in ten. I, indeed, affirm (and I fhall argue the right hereafter) that *every* man, and every *woman*, and every *child*, ought to obtain fomething more, in the general diftribution of the fruits of labour, than food, and rags, and a wretched hammock, with a poor rug to cover it : and that without working twelve or fourteen hours a day, fix days out of feven, from fix to fixty.—They have a claim, a facred and inviolable claim, growing out of that fundamental maxim, upon which alone all property can be fupported, to fome comforts and enjoyments, in addition to the neceffaries of life ; and to fome " tolerable

" tolerable leifure for fuch difcuffion, and fome
" means of fuch information," as may lead to an
underftanding of their *rights*; without which they
can never underftand their *duties*. It is true,
in the prefent circumftances of fociety, the mafs
of the people are far from the enjoyment of
this right : let Mr. B. determine whether this is
to be attributed to the nature, or the corruption
of our inftitutions. But ftill, notwithftanding the
fcandaloufly inadequate price of labour—wages
being, in many inftances, rather a mockery than
a fupport ;—notwithftanding the unreafonable
number of hours through which the labour of
the day is protracted, and the impediments
thrown in the way of a cheap, and, therefore
general, circulation of knowledge, by the duties
on paper, ftamps on news-papers, advertifements,
and the like; yet, judging of the whole country,
from the parts which I have feen, and making all
poffible allowances for the difference of local
and adventitious advantages, Mr. B. will not be
able to contract his *new ariflocracy of thinkers and
difcourfers* into any thing like the narrow circle of
four hundred thoufand. This champion for the
few, to the exclufion of the many—this advocate for the noble and the gentle, at the expence
of the ufeful and the honeft, may exult as much
as he pleafes in the luxuriancy of his imagination,
his various ftores of learning and of fcience, his

D 2   hours

hours of literary leifure, and his familiar intercourfe with the wits and literati of half a century, but there are hundreds, nay thoufands, in
thofe claffes excluded from his calculation, who
though they could neither endite, nor com-
prehend his learned metaphors and dafhing periods, would yet blufh at fuch flimfy fophifms as
he fometimes covers with a cloud of fplendour;
and with the weapons of plain, folid, Socratic
argument, would beat half a dozen fuch comba-
tants out of the arena. I could point him to
whole companies, whole neighbourhoods *, nay,

* I might refer particularly to Sheffield. My ftay in that
place was very fhort; but it was long enough to fee that there
is a great body of virtue, intelligence, and well grounded principle among what may be called the *Sanfculotterie :* but it is a
body without a head. They have unfortunately no leaders.
There are, indeed, feveral people of confiderable property and
influence who *think* with them; but who have not the courage,
or the energy, to take that open and decided part which might
promote the real peace (for *oppreffion is not peace)* and happinefs
of the neighbourhood : and as for that *Chicken-witted thing* that
calls *itfelf* a Whig leader in thofe parts, *it* is the being moft defpifed for ariftocratic domination of any creature in the county :
and I am fure I mean no difparagement to *Squire, Juftice, Colonel*
Aythorpe !!! If any three or four perfons of weight and
pecuniary confequence in that place, would but take thefe honeft, intelligent manufacturers and their caufe fairly and
publicly by the hand (as perfons of that defcription, to their
immortal honour, have done in Norwich) in Sheffield, as in
Norwich, the petty tyranny of provincial perfecution would
prefently be at an end; the inftruments of power would feel,
and practically confefs that falutary awe of which I have
fpoken above; and no jack in office would dare to exercife,
or to threaten, the exertion of a vigour beyond the law.

almoft

almoft whole profeffions of labouring manufacturers, who underftand the principles of government much better than himfelf, and who want
nothing but pra&ical fluency to render them
moft formidable antagonifts to the whole college
of ariftocratical declaimers.

The fa& is, that monopoly, and the hideous ac-
cumulation of capital in a few hands, like all difeafes not abfolutely mortal, carry, in their own
enormity, the feeds of cure. Man is, by his very
nature, focial and communicative—proud to difplay the little knowledge he poffeffes, and eager,
as opportunity prefents, to encreafe 'nis ftore.
Whatever preffes men together, therefo re, though
it may generate fome vices, is favoura ble to the
diffufion of knowledge, and ultimately promotive
of human liberty. Hence every larg e workfhop
and manufa&ory is a fort of politi cal fociety,
which no a& of parliament can file nce, and no
magiftrate difperfe. Socrates, there! fore, (the firft
democratical le&urer, mentioned in hiftory,
and the founder of the unfophiftice ted, and un-
reftri&ed fyftem of *Sanf-culotte* philofo phy) when he
wifhed to expofe " the corruption and venality
" of the times *," and thofe " falfe te nets and opi-
" nions which were contrary to the : happinefs of
" the human race †," a&ed confift ently with his

* Cullen's life of Socrates, prefixed to his tranflation of
the Phædon, p. 23.

† Ibid. p. 15.

high

high character for wifdom and penetration, in
vifiting, among other places of refort, the fhops
where workmen affembled to purfue their voca-
tions *.—" He began," fays the biographer, " to
" oppofe *fophiftry* and fuperftition with fuccefs,
" and to teach his fellow *citizens* wifdom and
" virtue. In the open ftreets, in the public
" walks and baths, in private houfes, in the *work-*
" *fhops of artifts,* or wherever he found men whom
" he could make better, he entered into converfa-
" tion with them, explained what was right and
" wrong, good and evil, holy and unholy, &c."
The nature and tendency of thefe converfations
we learn from a variety of paffages. We are particularly informed that fuch was his intrepid zeal
for the promotion of truth, and the affertion of
human liberty, that " As foon as any opinion or
" fuperftition occafioned an *open violence,* the in-
" vafion of the NATURAL RIGHTS OF
" MAN, or the corruption of their morals, no
" threats or perfecution could deter him from de-
" claring againft it †." And, again, we find that
when a fenate of tyrants, a vile and deteftable
Oligarchy ‡, affifted by an armed force, and a foreign alliance, trampled on the rights and liberties
of the Athenian people, and exercifed an authority beyond the law—" robbing the moft up-
" right men of the republic of their property and

* Life Socr. p. 12.   † Ibid. p. 32.   ‡ Ibid. p. 35.

" their

" their lives, *under the pretext of punishing rebellion and*
" *treasonable offences* *," banishing others, and driv-
ing many more to seek for peace and safety in voluntary emigration ; in the midst of these persecu-
tions and proscriptions, Socrates was found, as
usual, in the places of public resort—in the work-
shops of the artists, and among the labourers in
their manufactories, uttering seditious allegories,
and condemning the desolating tyranny of the
Oligarchy. " It is wonderful indeed," he is reported to have said, " if shepherds make the herd
" which is entrusted to their care grow smaller,
" and more meagre, and yet shall not be ac-
" counted bad shepherds ; but it is still more
" wonderful, if the guardians of a state make its
" subjects grow fewer and worse, that they should
" not be accounted bad guardians †."

Now,

---

* Cullen's Life of Socr. p. 35. *N. B.* The book from which
I quote this, was dedicated to the Right Honourable *Henry
Dundas,* in 1789.

† Ibid. p. 36. The reader will not, after these specimens, be
surprised that an act of parliament was made by the tyrannical
Oligarchy to stop the mouth of Socrates; and that *Critias* and
Characles, two of their sophists, or state lawyers *(see p.* 36.)
were employed to entrap, impeach, and destroy him; while
their buffoons were set to work, to ridicule and defame him to
the people, and " the *priests,*" and other venal wretches, " who
" felt Socrates a thorn in their side," made use of their pious
cant and holy mummeries " to turn the minds of the Athe-
" nians against him." *(p.* 24, 25.) Such was the origin of the
conspiracy against Socrates. A victim to that conspiracy he

fell

Now, though every workſhop cannot have a Socrates within the pale of its own ſociety, nor even every manufacturing town a man of ſuch wiſdom, virtue, and *opportunities* to inſtruct them, yet a ſort of Socratic ſpirit will neceſſarily grow up, wherever large bodies of men aſſemble. Each brings, as it were, into the common bank his mite of information, and putting it to a ſort of circulating uſance, each contributor has the advantage of a large intereſt, without any diminution of capital.

But ſuch men, I ſhall be told, are out of the queſtion : let their capacities, their acquirements, their underſtandings be what they may, they form no part of " the Britiſh public ;" they are in a ſtate of " menial *dependance* (or what is vir-" tually ſuch.)"—Dependance and independance! Fine diſtinctions! But in what do they conſiſt?

---

fell—the wiſeſt, the greateſt, the moſt virtuous of mankind. Yet a pedantic fellow, one Dr. Biſſet, in a certain ridiculous farrago of ignorance and miſrepreſentation, which he calls a " Sketch of Democracy," repreſents him as the victim of democratic envy and injuſtice ; and, by a curious perverſion of facts, makes *Critias* and *Characles* (the two ſophiſts, or lawyers, employed by the tyrants to deſtroy him) " two lecturers, who earned their bread by gratifying the prejudices of the people, and incenſing them againſt *dignified* characters." Socrates was ſo far from being a dignified character in Dr. B.'s ſenſe of the word, that his mother was a poor midwife ; his father a ſtone-maſon ; and he himſelf worked ſeveral years in his father's yard. His dignity was of a nobler kind.

Are

Are they to be fought in the ftation, or in the mind? Do wealth and rank give independance? Does induftrious poverty of neceffity degrade the man? An anecdote fhall fettle thefe queftions.

During the late election at Nottingham, one of the principal manufacturers of that place, who had always deprecated, with great feverity, the prefent war, and the whole fyftem of minifterial meafures, was obferved, of a fudden, to become referved and wavering. The minifterial candidate had concerns with a banking houfe, which, by means of acceptances, difcounts, and the like, was exceedingly ufeful to him, in his large dealings. Dr. *Crompton* was a candidate for the people: but he had no connection with any bank, but that of virtue and patriotifm; and their notes, you know, are not current in commercial tranfactions. The wealthy manufacturer deliberated —he doubted—he calculated—he refolved to vote for the minifterial champion. He determined to canvafs for him. " William," faid he, to one of his journeymen, " I hope you mean " to vote for Mr. *Smith?*"—" No, Sir," replied the *menial dependant*, " indeed I do not. I am fur- " prifed *you* fhould afk me fuch a queftion. How- " ever, if *you* are not independent, I AM!" This, however, I am aware, will be no argument, *ad ho- minem*, as they call it, to Mr. B. It will rather enflame than moderate his prejudices. He will re-

E gard

gard it as a flagrant act of *Jacobinifm* and infub-
ordination; an overt-act of treafon againft the
fovereignty of wealth; a " revolt of enterprifing
" talent againft property *."

I grant, alfo, that this argument will not uni-
verfally apply. Though fome men have energy of
mind enough to act in this independant way, upon
fuch occafions, many, under fuch circumftances,
feel themfelves compelled to bow. During the
fame Nottingham election, an inftance of this
fort occurred, which, to minds of a particular
ftamp at leaft, cannot fail to be interefting.

A poor manufacturer, who was paft his beft
days, and to whom, therefore, it was of ferious
confequence to be difmiffed from an eftablifhed
fhop—efpecially as he had a large family to fupport—was preffed by his employer, in very authoritative terms, to vote for this fame Mr. Smith.
He hefitated : but the very fuftenance of his family was at ftake; and he yielded. Going up
to the huftings, and having given in his name, he
was afked by the poll-clerk, for whom he voted?
" Why, I have two votes; have I not ?"—" You
" have."—" Well, then, I give one of them to
" Mr. Smith—but that's not mine: it's my maf-
" ter's! The other's my own; and I'll give that to
" Dr. Crompton—for he's the man for the peo-

* Letters, p. 93.

" ple!"

" ple !"—" Thank you, my good friend," (ex‑
claims the *courtly* candidate)—" thank you, for
" me. Let me have the pleasure of shaking
" hands with you."—No, I'm d—d if I do," re‑
plied the voter ; " I was obliged to vote for you,
" but I an't obliged to shake hands with you,
" neither. But I'll shake hands with you, Dr.
" Crompton; for I gave it *you* from my heart !"
Mr. B. may despise the sans-culotism displayed
in this anecdote—and I am certainly no enemy
to soothing manners and decorum ;—but yet
such energy of mind, however rudely fashioned,
is of ten thousand times more real worth than all
the polished periods of pensioned apostacy, and all
" the dressed up smiles that ever flickered on the
" curled lips" of obsequious courtiers ! And
whatever sentiments a master of the ceremonies
might entertain upon the subject, he is but a
shallow politician who excludes such men from
the account, in his calculations of the weight and
force of opinion. Such men have not, it is true,
all the advantages of free agency :—so much the
worse for Britain *. The generality of them have
no votes at all ; and many who have, are under
coercion in the exercise of their privilege—so

---

* I do not mean the mysterious, allegorical thing, which
statesmen call the country. I mean the aggregate of British
population. That is my idea of a country, or a state.

much

much the greater fcandal to juftice and humanity.
But though they have not votes, they have opinions. They are a part of " the Britifh public,"
even of Mr. Burke's *informed, difcuffing*, garrulous
public, upon which " more than the legal con-
ftituent, the artificial reprefentative," is fuppofed
(falfely fuppofed) to depend†. An oppreffive

---

† Letters, p. 67.
I ought not, while fpeaking of humble patriotifm, to forget
the *independant, poor* voters of Norwich : among which there
are fix or feven hundred, whom (even in thefe feafons of diftrefs) no threats, no intereft, no bribery can fhake : but who
will vote for the permanent liberties of themfelves and families, at the hazard of their temporary bread. Upon any *ftrong
exigency*, this number (I mean, among the *labouring freemen* of
that city) would be nearly doubled : that is to fay, it would
embrace almoft the whole clafs. If *Bartlet Gurney*, the
late candidate, had ftood forward manfully (or rather, if his
family had not held him back)—if he had even done thofe
things, which, under *exifting circumftances*, any candidate may
fairly and honourably do—I mean, brought up the London
and other out-voters, who were in his intereft, (which would
not have been the tythe, or twentieth part of what his oppo-
nent is *known* to have done)—nay, had he even fhewn himfelf
on the huftings, and convinced the people, that he was in ear-
neft, (inftead of *running into the north* to avoid them) he would
have driven the War Secretary from the market-place, with a
majority fo decifive, as would have funk that *bluftering puppet of
a day* into political annihilation. Even as it was, Bartlet Gurney
had a majority of 143 *refident votes.* The Quakers (that body of
men, whom, of all religionifts, I moft revere and love) muft
pardon me, if I fay, that the timid bafhfulnefs of fectarian
pride loft Freedom a triumph, of which no other circumftance
could have deprived her.

combination

combination of employers, the cold grafp of penury, or the brutal violence of a mad-headed,
drunken, profligate magiftrate (armed, for the
fake of the conftitutional fyftem of checks, with
the united powers of the police, and of the
fword) may fupprefs, for awhile, the due influence of this opinion ; but, ultimately, it will have
its weight : and its weight will be greateft when
its exertion is of moft importance.   In the mean
time, it has a degree of influence even now;
though not in its natural and rightful place—
that affembly which *calls itfelf* the Commons
Houfe of Parliament ;—the honourable and right
honourable members of which (as we are exprefsly told) are in fuch a ftate of " menial de-
" pendance, (or what is *virtually* fuch) that the
" *votes* of the majority are directly oppofite to
" their *difpofitions* *.   But it has its influence—a
powerful influence, upon the refources of the
country ; upon the expence and the facility of
filling the ranks of the army, and upon the fpirit
of enthufiafm in the day of battle.   It has its influence, alfo, on the pillow of the minifter, where
it requires no fecond-fight to perceive, that it
haunts his imagination, and difturbs his flumbers.
There, in prophetic vifions, it foretels the fad cataftrophe of his ambition, and points out, in the

* Letters, p. 63; and Thoughts, p. 14, where it is put ftill
more ftrongly.

continuance

continuance of this war, the means of Britifh renovation; the approaching failure of the funding
fyftem; the demurs of money-lenders, and the
prudent defertion of thofe " life and fortune
" men," who, repenting the madnefs of " Mer-
" chant Taylors Hall," and finding the bankrupt
ftate no longer competent to fupport, at once,
the burthen of public credit, and the enormous
prodigality of the prefent fyftem, will be obliged
to *abandon the borough-mongers to preferve their property.*

To appeafe this opinion, to lay this wandering
ghoft* of popular difcontent, the fimulator, Pitt,
has drawn once more around him this magic
circle of delufion, with charms and fpells of pretended negociation, and backward mutters of ar-
rogance and recantation. But lift up your voices,
ye artificers, ye mechanics, ye manufacturers of the
land, ye genuine props and pillars of the nation!
Be not amufed with pretended treaties! for what
is a peace but war, to you, while ye drudge in
fervile mifery for inadequate rewards, and your
families pine in want and ignorance? Wear not

---

* The body is reported to have been buried, at the beginning of December laft, in St. Stephen's Chapel, with this
infcription—" Pitt and Grenville's Acts;"—and underneath,
" in a ftate of *internal tranquillity.*" Thus much by authority.
To which is added, by an unknown hand, " but in hopes of a
" joyful refurrection."

your

your lungs with fighs and fullen murmurs—let not only the nocturnal phantom, but the living body of your complaints appear before your oppreffors. Try once more the manly energies of reafon; and tell them, with a clear and decided tone, that " peace is not peace, without re-" form :" that " your difcontents can never be " allayed, without the reftoration of equal rights, " and equal laws, and the adoption of a pure and " independant organ, through which the opinions, " not of a *tenth-part*, but of the whole nation, " can be freely delivered, and diftinctly heard."

But no : we are told, the nation wants no fuch organ. The opinions of the *menial*, *dependant mafs*, muft be taken for granted from thofe of their *betters*. In thofe more reputable orders, in that privileged four hundred thoufand, who, by virtue of their fituation, have an exclufive licence to enquire and. to difcufs, the people have, already, " a *natural* reprefentative." Natural reprefentative !—Of what excellent ufe, in the fcience of confufing mankind, is this prerogative of coining new phrafes ! Natural reprefentative of the people! The people itfelf, as the word is here ufed, is an artificial, or corporate body—for it means the aggregate population of a particular ftate, or body politic : and how there can be a *natural representative* of an *artificial corporation*, I am yet to learn. I can underftand, indeed, that the parent

is

is the natural reprefentative of his infant children, armed with the right, and bound by the duty of judging and acting for them. I can, alfo, under-ftand, that children are the natural reprefentatives of a departed parent; and, as fuch, are entitled to thofe portions of the produce of his labour, which have neither been confumed by him, nor legally fet apart to fupport the profligate luxury of placemen and penfioners. But how it fhould happen, that four hundred thoufand people *(men and women)* from the mere *accident* of living in more comfort, and with lefs toil, fhould be the natural reprefentatives of three or four millions of other full-grown—full-aged beings, of the fame ftruéture and faculty with themfelves, but to whom they have neither relationfhip nor affinity, and, as fuch, fhould be entitled to act for them, fpeak for them, think for them, and almoft eat for them (for even this privilege is fcarcely left to the perfonal exercife of the million) is a pro-blem which the " jurifts and publicifts" muft folve; for I give it up entirely.

But Mr. B.'s *nature* and mine are widely different. With him every thing is natural that has the hoar of ancient prejudice upon it ; and novelty is the teft of crime. In my humble eftimate, no-thing is natural, but what is fit and true, and can endure the teft of reafon. With him the feudal fyftem, and all its barbarous, tyrannical, and

and fuperftitious appendages, is natural. With
him, all the gaudy, cumbrous, fuftian of " the
" old Germanic, or Gothic cuftumary" is natural, and all the idolatrous foppéry and degrading
fuperftition of the church of Rome are natural,
alfo: Nay, with him, that deteftable traffic in
blood and murder—that barter of groans, and
tortures, and long, long lingering deaths of fhriek-
ing anguifh, the *Slave Trade*, is alfo natural.
Nor do I doubt, that, with equal facility, and
upon the very fame principles, as he maintains
the mafters and employers of this country to be
the natural reprefentatives of the workmen they
employ, he could prove, alfo, thofe very humane,
and very, very refpeĉtable beings, who, as they
walk upon two legs, I fhall continue to call men,
by *courtefy*, (I mean the Weft India Planters, and
their Negro drivers) to be the natural reprefentatives of thofe poor, haraffed, half-ftarved, whip-
galled, miferable flaves, whom they, alfo, *employ*
in their farms and faĉtories.

In fhort, this champion of the privileged orders
adopts, moft unequivocally, the principle of this
fimilitude. Having affigned the exclufive privilege
of opinion to the favoured four hundred thoufand—a mixed herd of nobles and gentles, placemen, penfioners, and court-expeĉtants, of bankers
and merchants, manufaĉturers, lawyers, parfons

F   and

and phyficians, warehoufemen and fhop-keepers,
pimps and king's meffengers, fiddlers and auc-
tioneers, with the included " twenty thoufand"
petticoat allies—ladies of the court, and ladies of
the town!—having fecured this motley groupe
(the favoured progeny of Means and Leifure) in
the exclufive, and unqueftioned enjoyment of
the rights of information and difcuffion, he proceeds to obferve, that " the reft, when feeble,
" are the *objects* of protection!"—Objects of protection!— fo are my lady's lap-dog and the
Negro flave. It is eafy to determine, which, of
the two, *polifhed fenfibility* will fhelter with the moft
anxious care!—Ye murky walls, and foul, ftraw-
littered floors of the plantation hofpital! Ye
full-crammed, noxious workhoufes of Britain—
vile dens of tyrannic penury and putrefcence*!
fpeak—fpeak, I charge ye (for that part of nature
which fhould be loud and eloquent, is fpell-bound
in panic apathy)—Speak: what is the *protection*
which the feeble labourer, or the fick Negro finds?
and then refer for a comparifon to the down
pillow of yon pampered, fnarling cur, or the commodious chambers of the canine palace at *God-*

---

* There are fome few, and but few exceptions, to this general
defcription. At any rate, however, a workhoufe is but a gaol;
and, therefore, a fit receptacle only for thofe paupers, whofe
infirmities make confinement neceffary to their prefervation.

wood.

wood *.—But to return to the defcription.—" The
" reft, when feeble, are the objeɛls of protεɛlion—
" when *ftrong*, they are the MEANS of force †."
So is the dray-horfe ; and the poor afs that drudges
in yon fand-cart! So are the bludgeon, and the
piftol, with which, under *exifting circumftances*, every
man (at leaft, every marked, obnoxious man) will
do well to be provided, as prefervatives againft affaffination ‡. But foul befal the man, and foul
befal the government, that confiders the great
mafs of the people as mere brute machines ; in-
fenfate inftruments of phyfical force, deprived of
all *power*, and deftitute of all *right* of reafon, or
information ; doomed, like the dray-horfe, or the
mufquet, to perform, mechanically, whatever tafk
of drudgery, or murder, a few " counfellers and
deliberators " may command ! And yet, Mr. B.

---

* A fplendid edifice, erεɛled by the D. of Richmond for
his dogs, with commodious kitchens, parlours, dining-rooms,
bed-rooms, lying-in-rooms, pleafure-ground for the morning
fun, pleafure-ground for the evening fun, baths, &c. &c.—
N. B. It is a ftriɛl rule at Godwood, that no fervant be
permitted to give a morfel of broken viɛluals either to mendi-
cant traveller, or neighbouring peafant. Poor women, who
prefume to pick up withered fticks from under the trees in
the park, are taught, by a " fevere and awful " adminiftration of " juftice," to refpeɛl the facred rights of property.

† Letters, p. 67.

‡ See an Appeal to Popular Opinion againft Kidnapping
and Murder; including a Narrative of the atrocious Outrages
at Yarmouth, Lynn, and Wifbech.—*Jordan*.

tells

tells us, that " they who *affect* to confider that
" part of us" (to wit, nine-tenths of the adult
population of the country) " in any other point
" of view, *infult while they cajole us* * !"

Such, my fellow-citizens, is the language of
infolence itfelf, perfonified in the character of a
penfioned proftitute? Nine out of ten of the human race (it will, anon, be nineteen out of
twenty) are born to be beafts of burthen to the
remaining tythe: to be hewers of wood, and
drawers of water—to be expofed to heat and
cold, winds and waters, rocks and tempefts, for
thefe privileged mafters ; and, finally, to be " lift-
" ed as foldiers for battle *," to defend, or to ag-
grandife a country, in which they have neither
voice nor right. And he who dares to affert their
claim to " any tolerable leifure for difcuffion, or
" means of information :"—he who dares to maintain their pretenfions to opinion, or title to be
regarded " in any political view," as a part of
" the people," is an hypocritical jacobin incen-
diary, revolts againft the fovereignty of wealth,
and " infults while he cajoles us!" Such is the
language of a man to whom our government
gives a yearly penfion of four thoufand pounds,
for diftracting the world with the ravings of bedlam, and the filthy loquacity of the ftews, in

* Letters, p 67.

favour

favour of ariftocratic defpotifm, and beating the tough hide of old Zifca, " to animate Europe to " eternal battle *!"

But beware, Mr. Burke, and you, his hypocritical employers, how *ye* cajole and infult *us* too far. Abufes, when difcovcred, infpire the fober wifh of peaceful and rational reform : but when wrong is added to wrong, and coercion to coercion ; when remonftrance is anfwered by the goad and the yoke, and infult is heaped upon oppreffion, reafon may be overpowered, and madnefs may fucceed ; and the philanthropic few, who admonifh in vain, may deplore the deftiny from which they cannot preferve you. In vain do you fhudder at the cannibals† of Paris—in vain do you colour, with exaggerated horrors, the " tribunals of Maroon and Negro flaves, covered " with the blood of their maflers ‡;" if, obftinately vicious, inftead of being warned, ye are irritated by the example.

I deplore, as you do, the " robberies and the " murders," of thefe poor wretches—the blind inftruments of inftinctive vengeance. But, I cannot, like you, forget by whom thofe leffons of

---

* Letter to a Noble Lord.

† The reader will, of courfe, give me credit, for ufing this word in a figurative fenfe. Mr. B. in the very dotage of credulity, applies it literally.

‡ Letters, p. 123. Thoughts, p. 61.

murderous

murderous rapacity were taught. I cannot forget, that flavery itfelf is robbery and murder; and, that the mafter who falls by the bondfman's hand, is the victim of his own barbarity.

I am no apologift for the horrible maffacres of revenge; whether perpetrated by negroes, by monarchs, or by mobs. I abhor revenge. Vengeance, Mr. Burke, with me is crime. All retrofpective principle is crime; and to its crime, adds folly. In your own fort of language I fhould fay—we were *made* with our eyes in our foreheads, that we might look onward to the future, not linger upon that which can never be recalled. Give me *fecurity for the future*, I will difpenfe with what is called *juftice for the paft*. But we are not to expect whole nations (whether of Maroon negroes, or vaffals of feudal tyranny) to become of a fudden fo entirely fpeculative. Revenge, it cannot be concealed, is a rude inftinct, common to all animated being, which nothing but deep reflection, and well digefted principles can eradicate. It is an inftinct, alfo, when it dares to fhew itfelf, ftrongeft in the moft feeble, fierceft in the moft fubmiffive, and moft fruitful in the fteril foil of ignorance. The bleak froft of feverity nourifhes it to wild luxuriance. It perifhes beneath the warm manure of kindnefs. It is a wild growth of nature, it is true: but it is fatally cherifhed by authoritative example: and if tyrants will teach

bloody

bloody leffons, it is unreafonable in them to complain of the aptitude of their fcholars. Add to
which, Mr. B. this *deteſtable vice* is one of the
virtues of the *ancient and venerable* part of that religion you fo anxioufly uphold. The maxim of
forgivenefs to enemies, is, comparatively, a *modern
innovation :* which accounts for its being fo feldom
practifed by governments or priefts. " Eye for
" eye, and tooth for tooth," will not fatisfy them.
Theirs are the dread inftructions, " which, being
" taught, return to plague the inventors." Theirs,
indeed, too generally, are the crimes unprovoked :
the crimes of revolutionifts are only the crimes
of revenge. Had the Maroons and negroes never
been moſt wickedly enſlaved, their maſters had
never been murdered. Had the chains of France
been lefs galling, they had never fallen fo heavy
on the heads of French oppreffers. To avoid
their fate, let governors avoid their crimes. To
render fanguinary *revolutions* impoſſible, let them
yield to temperate *reforms.* To avert a dreaded
vengeance, let the provocations of injuſtice be
inſtantly removed ; and the padlock from the
mouth of an injured people, be transferred to
the lips of penſioned infolence !

But the politician of Beaconsfield, " the doc-
" tor of the conftitution"—or rather the doctor's
doctor, has found a fhorter way.—" The cautery

" and

" and the knife" are more fovereign than the
emollient and the balm. Extermination (even
of eighty thoufand men of talent and capacity)
is more eafy than reform. Defolation itfelf is
not to minifterial ears " a word of fuch ill found"
as " change ;" and Jacobins and reformers are
therefore to be fubmitted to the " fevere and
" awful operation," in a manner that will expofe
" the crown" to no fort of danger of again " re-
" tiring difgraced and defeated from its courts."

" Of thefe four hundred thoufand *political citi-*
" *zens,*" fays he, " I look upon one-fifth, or about
" eighty thoufand, to be *pure Jacobins* ; *utterly in-*
" *capable of amendment* ; objects of eternal vigi-
" lance," &c. " On thefe, no reafon, no argu-
" ment, no *example*, no *venerable authority*, can
" have the flighteft influence. They defire"—
What ? " A *change* ; and they will have it if they
" can."—True : And they ought to have it ; and
they muft, or the nation is undone for ever. If all
are Jacobins who wifh for a change, Mr. B. moft
miferably under-rates the Jacobins of this country. Some wifh for a greater change, and others
for a lefs. There are, I fear, almoft as many different opinions, among reformers, as to the extent of that change, as there were among the allies about the objects of that ever to be renowned
and glorious confederacy of kings, by being chief

trumpeter

trumpeter to which—or, more properly fpeaking, drum-major (for we muſt not forget old Zifca) Mr. Burke has accumulated ſo conſiderable a portion of ſpoil, at ſo ſmall an expence of danger. But, barring the idle terrors which ſtate jugglers keep ſo alertfully alive, by repeating, at due intervals, and with due ſolemnity, the cabaliſtic words, *French maſſacres ! republicans and levellers ! horrid atheiſts ! dreadful anarchy ! bloody regicides ! cannibal philoſophy !* and the like, I believe there is ſcarcely a ſingle reflecting man, unconnected, by intereſt or expectation, with exiſting corruptions, who does not, in ſome degree, wiſh a change. But ſays Mr. B. " England has been happy ; and " change is a word of ill ſound to happy ears*."— England *has been* happy!!!—Perhaps ſo. England was not always infeſted with ſuch a peſtiferous ſwarm of placemen and penſioners, boroughmongers and contractors, as, at this time, devour the harveſts, and blaſt the ſmiling verdure of the year. Will Mr. B. pretend to ſay, that England *is* happy now ? Will he pretend to ſay, that even that ſmall portion, that tythe, which he calls " the Britiſh public," are happy at this time ? And if they were, what

---

* Thoughts, p. 1.—In Rivington's edition this is omitted. A qualm of modeſty ſeems, unaccountably, to have ſeized the author, and this inſult to our feelings was ſtruck out. But, thanks to Mr. Owen ! (honourable mention of him in the journals of political literature !) we have the firſt thoughts, as well as the after thoughts. Of the writings of Burke we can never have too much.

right has a tenth part to be happy at the expence of the mifery of all the reft? But, can even thefe be called happy? Are thofe middle claffes (which we middling people are apt, fo felfifhly, and fo wickedly, to confider as the whole!)—are even they happy? Alas! alas! how difmal the re-verfe?

Ye tradefmen, ye manufacturers, ye noifelefs proficients in the arts, the fciences, and the gainful branches of learning 'the bulk and mafs of all thofe callings and profeffions *nick-named* RESPECTABLE*) tell me—tell *the world*, can ye look in the innocent faces of your children, and, contemplating the profpect before them, fay, that ye are happy? Can ye look upon your own con-dition, your blighted profpects, and your ftinted comforts, and, even barring future profpects, fay ye are happy? Alas! how many of you are, at this very time, defcending, and how rapidly, down the ladder of degradation! A few (I grant it) profper. A few fwell to uncontroulable pride, and incal-culable affluence. The more is your difafter. To be, like Tantalus, in a lake of mifery, with the profpect of abundance conftantly before our eyes, and never tafte it, is to be doubly loft. But what is the condition of the mafs?—*Your*

* Refpect is not the attribute of property, calling, or con-dition. It belongs, in reality, to nothing but virtue; and to that which is a branch of virtue—well applied talents.

little

little mafs, I mean.   As for *the great mafs*—it
is trampled in the duft; and is forgotten.   How
many of you have been obliged to relinquifh your
little country houfe, or country lodging ?—fweet
recreations of health and pleafure ! which at once
prolonged exiftence, and decked it with a ruddier
fmile ! From the tables of how many has the tax-
gatherer fnatched the cheering wine ? How many,
many a family, that once bafked in the inner, has
been pufhed to the outer circles of this temperate
zone? How many from thefe outer circles have been
thruft into the chill regions of penurious labour ?
And, how many thoufands, upon whofe moderate
toil the fidelong fun once caft his cheering gleams,
now fhiver at the dark, bleak poles of comfortlefs diftrefs ?

If, then, our happinefs be reduced to a mere
" has been," this terrible *change*, is the burthen
of *a dirge*, rather than a *word of omen* ; and muft
imprefs us rather with plaintive than terrific fen-
fations.   We might, therefore, with ftrict propriety difmifs the fubject, in Mr. B's own ftyle,
by declaring that the objection " will not apply ;
" and put it out of court accordingly : ordering,
" that fo far as that goes, the counfel for exifting
" abufes take nothing by his motion *."

But the counfel in this caufe is a deep politi-

* Letters, p. 129.

G 2   cian.

cian. He can practice popular arts againſt the
people. His motion was not made with any view
to the deciſion of that high court of reaſon, to
which he appealed, but for the ſake of the general impreſſion expected from the mere motion itſelf. Change is a word of ambiguous meaning ;
and, under certain circumſtances, the worſt
conſtruction is ſure to be put upon every am-
biguity. It ſhould be remembered, therefore,
that *change, revolution*, and *reform*, are but mo-
difications of the ſame idea : though the laſt,
by eſtabliſhed courteſy, is the moſt unequivocally admitted in a favourable ſenſe. *Reform* is a
change, or *revolution, from bad to good.* Every
uſurpation, and every conceſſion, is a change.
Every alteration of the law, the repeal of an old
act, or the paſſing of a new one, is a change. The
whole hiſtory of government is nothing but a re-
cord of changes, or revolutions, gradual or ſud-
den ; and the worſt revolutions are thoſe that
are never called ſo. In ſhort, abſtractedly conſi-
dered, there is nothing terrible in change or revolution. Violence and cruelty are to be abhorred.
Humanity is to be loved and cheriſhed. Firſt and
greateſt of all virtues ! parent of all bleſſings !
fountain of all ſocial joys ! it is to be wooed, and
foſtered, and reverenced with the fondeſt care !
to be claſped to the breaſt, and entwined with the
very texture of the heart—only to be torn away
with

with the laſt, deareſt fibre. But when violence
and cruelty are eſtabliſhed—when they are ſur-
rounded by privileges, and fortified by power,
revolution itſelf becomes humanity and juſtice.

The queſtion, then, is, what ſort of a change
do we deſire? Does Mr. B. mean to ſay, that
one-fifth of the people of that claſs which he regards as " the Britiſh public," *deſires a change* of
tumult, ferocious anarchy and ſlaughter?—O
woeful Britain! if this were indeed the caſe:
for there would ſcarcely be a paper partition between thee and the flames of the moſt hideous
deſolation. But if, by change, he means, as I do,
redreſs of grievances, and reform of long-growing
corruptions, I repeat it, not a fifth, but four-fifths
of the thinking part of the community, do, in their
hours of ſanity, when the tertian of alarm ſubſides,
wiſh for ſuch a change : and when I look around
on the condition of my country, and the ſcan-
dalous abuſes of government, proud am I to be
confidered, among the diſtinguiſhed eighty thouſand, not the leaſt obnoxious to Mr. B. and his
new employers.

After having thus indulged his indolence, in a
little faint and dubious colouring, the artiſt, however, preſently returns to his *old daſhing ſtyle.* " If
" they cannot have this change, which they de-
" ſire, by Engliſh cabal," ſays he, " they will
" make

make no fort of fcruple of having it by the ca-
" bal of France, into which already they are *vir-*
" *tually incorporated.*" Thus, *all reformers* are Jacobins; and all Jacobins are of the French faction,
virtually incorporated with that nation, and willing
to fecure the change they wifh by foreign interference.

As for *virtual incorporation,* or *virtual prefence,*
whether in a *wafer,* or a *confederacy,* they are myf-
teries which, I profefs, I do not underftand. Mr.
B. perhaps could explain the one, and fome of
our good allies might write commentaries on the
other. But I am not curious about occult fciences;
and I fhall only obferve, that if the French republic derives no greater benefit from our *virtual incorporation* than the grand confederacy from the
virtual co-operation of the Emprefs of Ruffia's
manifeftoes, it would be moft gratuitous prodigality in government to be at any further expence
for fpecial commiffions, and trials for high treafon.
For my own part, at leaft, I have no objection to
avow all the incorporation I am confcious of with
French Jacobinifm.

I do confefs, that fo long as I imagined it even
poffible for the republic to be overthrown, no
profpect was accompanied with equal anguifh.
For, notwithftanding the many adventitious
horrors which have clouded the revolution, I regarded it as a great and glorious effort for the
emancipation

emancipation and moral improvement of the human race. But the thought has long ceafed to agitate my mind. The Republic ftands upon a rock; and Æolus may blow till he cracks his cheeks, but all the blafts of his eloquence will never fhake it. We muft have miracles; or all is fafe. " The fluices of heaven muft be " opened, and the waters of the great deep be " broken up;" for nothing lefs than a general deluge can deftroy it.

As for Englifh reform by foreign cabal, I fhall only obferve, that I hold, with refpect to England, the fame doctrines that I held with refpect to France. I deny Mr. B.'s law of vicinage altogether; and fhall reply to his fophifms in another letter. In the mean time, I would have the reformers of all nations keep for ever in their minds the monitory remembrance, that hatred may be forced, but love cannot; that chains may be *impofed*, but freedom muft be *acquired.*—In other words, that no country can have freedom, which cannot obtain it for itfelf; and that *foreign interference can only, at beft, produce a change of mafters* *.

* This maxim, however, applies only to thofe nations in which foreign mercenaries are not employed by the government. It is no impeachment of the conduct of the Dutch. They were, already, under a foreign yoke. Their government coerced them by Britifh and Pruffian mercenaries; and they had no choice but that of accepting the aid of French fraternity.

But,

But, this is by the way. All I have to do, at prefent, with Mr. B.'s charge, is, to fhew the point of view in which he regards, or pretends to regard, the opinions of eighty thoufand of thofe people of Britain, who, by virtue of their pecuniary fituations, *are licenced to think on politics.* This, together with what he fays of the talents and capacities of thefe men, will form the firft branch of what I fhall venture to call *Burke's new fyllogifm of maffacre.*

" I have a good opinion," fays he, " of the ge-
" neral abilities of the Jacobins."—In his very laft publication, they were a herd of " fools
" afpiring to be knaves*;" and the reader cannot have forgotten his vehement declamations at the beginning of the conteft with France, againft
" the vileft, the moft defpicable, the moft igno-
" rant of mankind ; who, unlike the Englifh Re-
" volutionifts of the laft century—for they were
" men of genius and intelligence—that was a
" ftruggle of talents for their natural afcendency
" —a transfer of power, from the ariftocracy of
" birth, to the ariftocracy of mind; but thefe men,
" on the contrary, had overthrown *all* diftinc-
" tions, and transferred dominion, not to the
" wifdom and the intellect, but to the folly and
" ignorance of the nation† !" But now, " I

---

* Letter to a Noble Lord.

† I have not the fpeech before me : but this, I know, was the ftrain and fentiment of that furious philippic.

" have

" have a good opinion of the general abilities
" of Jacobins." Who knows, but that bye-and-
by, he may take another turn, and entertain a
good opinion of their principles? Change is with
him no inconfiftency. · Mr. B. and the weather-
cock, are only out of character when they are
fixed. " Strong paffions," fays he, " awaken the
" faculties. *They* fuffer not a particle of the
" man to be loft. The fpirit of enterprife gives
" to this defcription the full ufe of all their na-
" tive energies *." And again, in his fecond
Letter †:—" It is a dreadful truth, but it is a
" truth that cannot be concealed ; in ability, in·
" dexterity, in the *diftinctnefs of their views, the*
" *Jacobins are our fuperiors.* They faw the thing
" right from the very beginning!!!" &c.—Such is·
the picture drawn by this fublime politician of that·
" great and formidable minority" (not, gentle
reader, the whig minority of the Houfe of Commons!) of whom he wifhes to put the men of
family and property in terror, that he may put
them into *blood.* To complete the picture, in the
true ftyle and colouring of alarm, he adds, " I do
" not know whether, if I aimed at the total over-

---

* Letters, p. 70. Thoughts, p. 20.
† Letters, p. 144. Thoughts, p. 87. Compare this with
his picture (Let. p. 145. Thoughts, p. 89) of " the tribe of
" vulgar politicians" that throng the courts of princes !!! and
who can doubt the iffue of the ftruggle?

H   " throw

" throw of a kingdom, I fhould wifh to be en-
" cumbered with a larger body of partizans.
" They are more eafily difciplined and directed,
" than if the number were greater *." Nay, and
fo difciplined, and fo directed does he conceive us
to be, that he afcribes to us a fort of omnipre-
fence, and fupernatural power of metamorphofis
—" paffing from place to place, with incredible
" velocity, and diverfifiying our character and de-
" fcription, fo as to be capable of mimicking the
" general voice! †"

And what has all this to do (you will naturally
enquire) with the argument againft a Regicide
Peace? Will the government, by exhaufting the
refources of the nation, be better enabled to
ftruggle againft fuch a faction (admitting its exiftence)? Will the increafe of burthens, the beggary, mifery, and confequent difcontents, growing out of the prolongation of war, make fuch a
faction lefs formidable? (Though not anxious myfelf for peace, I argue the queftion openly and
fairly. In cafes fo momentous, there ought to
be no difguife.) Would the unthinking, the
defperate, the fickle and the wavering, be the
lefs likely to fall into the hands, and be rendered
inftrumental to the views of fuch men, from the
accumulating miferies, which, from fuch pro-

* Letters, p. 68. Thoughts, p. 18. † Ibid.

longation,

longation, muft inevitably refult? Mr. B. is not
fuch an ideot as to believe it. His hyperbolical
ftatement might, indeed, fupernaturally account
for a general *exclamâtion*, without admitting a general *defire*, for peace: fuppofing, indeed, that
fuch *general* exclamation had been raifed. But
this I deny. The moderates (the patchwork-
men—place-hunters, and dupes of place-hunters)
wifh for peace, I believe; and fuch of the mo-
nied men as have no advantage from loans and
contracts, or as dread the confequences of a frefh
loan: but as for the Jacobins—indeed, Mr. Burke,
(maugre all your profound penetration) they are
very indifferent about the matter: they know
(as you do) that peace, under *exifting circumftances*,
could only be a hollow truce *: that the over-
burthened labourer would ftill continue to be
taxed for enormous fums to be fquandered in
foreign intrigue, to difturb the tranquillity, and
irritate the government of France; and that
" what now *ftands for* a government" in England,

---

* Since this was written, I have feen a fpirited and well-
written pamphlet, " *Utrum Horum* : — The Government, or
the Country," in which this idea is further purfued; and the
diftinction between a *real* peace, and a peace concluded by *our*
prefent government, is ably marked. D. O'Brien—I obferve,
with pleafure, he has not daubed his title-page either with *Mr.*
or *Efq.*—D. O'Bryen, and myfelf, differ upon fome points—
our habits, and, perhaps, our objects, are fomewhat diffimular:
but different mediums do not prevent us from feeing the fame
great glaring truths.

I mean

(I mean Pitt and Hawkefbury's difcordant cabal)
has injured the French Republic too outrageoufly
ever to forgive it. In fhort, they know that there is
no peace for Europe, fo long as the unnatural alliance between the funding fyftem and the borough-mongering fyftem lafts; and that, therefore,
any thing (in how queftionable a fhape foever it
may come) would be, ultimately, a blefling, that
fhould bring this unnatural alliance to the crifis
of a divorce. Sooner or later, this crifis, I believe, muft come : and when it does come, " Pe-
" rifh, the Borough-mongers," I fay, for one,
" and let the public creditor be fecured!"—In
other words, let corruption be deftroyed—let
plunderers and ruffians be difmiffed from power,
let penfions be abolifhed, finecures be totally
abrogated, and the falaries of all offices reduced
to a level with the mere neceffary expences of
the table and the library, of a man of fcience and
public bufinefs : Let fimplicity and virtue be fub-
ftituted for oftentatious debauchery ; and thus
let the peafant and the manufacturer be redeemed
from mifery ; and, at the fame time, the thoufands, and tens of thoufands of virtuous families,
whofe *well-earned competence* is now vefted in government fecurities, be preferved from hideous
ruin. Thus it is, and only thus, that the joint
object can be attained, and the jarring interefts

of

of the ftock-holder, and the produ&ive labourer, be united.

But if Mr. B.'s extravagant picture of Britifh Jacobinifm has nothing to do with the argument on Regicide Peace, it has fomething to do with that which is of infinitely more importance: it has fomething to do with our palladium, Trial by Jury: it has fomething to do with all the yet-remaining fences of our little, little liberty—with all that ftands between the head of the patriot and the axe of minifterial vengeance.

But take it not upon credit. Truft not to my affertion. Read the book yourfelves—or rather the books: for the parts in which they differ, and the parts in which they agree, are equally important to the juft difplay of the temper and views with which they were compofed. Confider the whole. Compare together the refpective parts; and if ever you execrate again the names of Robefpierre and Marat, without glowing with fuperior deteftation for Edmund Burke, it is only, becaufe it is in the nature of man, that reafon fhould be the fool of imagination, and that guilt fhould lofe its guiltinefs in our eyes, when impotence prevents the perpetration of its malice.

Hear, for example, his affected lamentations over " the total relaxation of all authority,"

" rity *," the " inefficiency of tribunals," the backwardnefs of whofe " moft effential members" (the juries, I fuppofe, he means) to execute the bloody mandates of a minifter, is defcribed, with infidious obfcurity, as a " difowning of the go- " vernment." See, alfo, his furious attack upon the Houfe of Lords, becaufe that " higheft tri- " bunal of all," would not indulge his rhetorical fpleen with the condemnation of Warren Haft. ings. There was no evidence, it is true : no cafe made out. But what of that? Mr. Burke can have no idea of " the reafon, and equity, and juf- " tice," of that " fevere and aweful—living law," to which he fo pompoufly appeals, unlefs trial and condemnation are one and the fame thing; and accufation, fentence, and execution follow each other with as mechanical a certitude as the conclufions of a mathematical problem refult from its premifes—Without this, it is " dead and " putrid ; infufficient to fave the ftate, but potent " to infect and to kill."

But " the very ftorm and tempeft of his rage," are referved for the *treafonable* acquittals—for trea- fon, it feems, it was, that we fhould be acquitted. That Lords and Commons fhould have joined to- gether in votes of prejudication—that Minifters

---

* Letters, p. 19, and 20. This is one of the additions, for the purpofe of working up which to due fublimity, the work has been kept fix months in the prefs.

and

and Crown Lawyers fhould have projeſted and
planned fuch elaborate profecutions; and twifted
and twined, and diftorted all law and common
fenfe, till the very ftatutes of the realm, and the
Englifh language itfelf, were turned infide out,
and logic and jurifprudence walked topfy-turvy,
like the captive king of the Antipodeans, in
Chrononhotonthologos—that his own moft fublime and *inventive* genius fhould have been employed in arranging, drawing out, garbelling and
embellifhing "Reports of Secret Committees *"—
that Courts of Special Commiffion fhould have
been adorned with fuch pomp and circumftance
—Bedlam, Bridewell, and the ftews, fo ranfacked
for collateral evidence,and nature's loofe analogies
explored for moonfhine links of unconnected faſts:
that Judges, Counfel, and Witneffes, fhould have
been fo well chofen, and fo well paid †, and Juries

fo

* This,is believed to be one of the *important fervices* for which
Mr. B. received that penfion of 4000l. a year, which he fo
modeftly affures us, " is no more than he deferved ! !"—*Letter
to a Noble Lord.*

† All the witneffes were not paid alike ; or with equal good
will. The honeft fellows from Sheffield were difmiffed with
the price of an outfide paffage on the coach, and about 7s. for
expences on a journey of 200 miles. My very valuable and
lamented friend, the late John Stuart Taylor, of Norwich,
when he applied to a certain gentleman in office, or Jack
in office, which ever you pleafe to call him, for thofe fixed and
regular expences, which the fubpoenaing party always pays, to
every profeffional man, during the time he is withheld from
his

fo carefully felected, with fuch due proportions on each pannel, of contractors, police magiftrates, and tradefmen to the royal family*; and yet, after all, that we fhould come off with our heads upon our fhoulders, and " the CROWN retire dif-" graced and defeated from ITS courts," with only the folitary, *ambiguous* confolation of execut-ing one of its own fpies—this

> " Is grief too fierce for nerves like his to bear,
> " And claims the horrors of a laft defpair!"

He raves till he foams again. Like a wounded elephant, his enemies having efcaped, he turns his fury upon his friends—upon himfelf—upon thofe very pavillions and edifices of ftate he was armed and caparifoned to defend ; and four dread pages † of fplendid ruins, are covered over with froth and blood.

---

his bufinefs, was anfwered with furly infolence—" Expences, " Sir—for fuch a witnefs as you! Do you think it was for " this you were brought up to London ? You were ex-" pected to give evidence on the part of the crown, not on " the part of the prifoner ! ! !"—When the Lynams, the Taylors, the Grovefes, the Timfes went for their *expences*, was there any demur ? ? ? No, they had faid all that was ex-pected—and almoft every word of it had been proved to be falfe.

* To the immortal honour of thofe men—to the honour of our national character, this was not a fufficient inducement to thofe honeft men to bring in a verdict for the crown againft the evidence.

† Letters, p. 19 to 22.

" The

" The higheſt tribunal of all is deprived of all
" dignity and efficiency."—" Public proſecutions
" are become little better than ſchools for trea-
" ſon ; of no uſe but to improve the dexterity of
" *criminals*" [i. e. *reformers*] " in the myſtery of *eva-*
" *ſion*," [i. e. *of avoiding the ſociety of perjured ſpies !*]
" to ſhew with what complete impunity men
" may conſpire againſt *the common* WEALTH,"
[that is to ſay, in plain Engliſh, againſt *the corrup-*
tions of a gang of borough-mongers—the PLUNDER
of a hord of placemen and penſioners !] " to ſhew
" with what ſafety *aſſaſſins* may attempt its awful
" head !"

There is a gradation, it ſeems, in *honourable*
obloquy : but ſurely we are now at the ladder's
top. Mr. Windham made us *white-waſhed felons ;*
Lord Grenville *ſtained us with moral guilt ;* and
Mr. B. has dubbed us ASSASSINS. It would be
curious to know what epithet this *Gentleman ! ! !*
would give to thoſe ruffians *(moſtly in the pay of*
Government) who were concerned in the meditated,
attempted maſſacres of Lynn and Yarmouth !—In
the mean time, I wonder how *juries* reliſh theſe
things. But it matters not. They are not to
be uſed any more, I ſuppoſe, *on ſuch occaſions.*

Having exhauſted his ſtock of Newgate wit,
the metaphorical Proteus now turns his hand to
medicine and ſurgery, and cures low fevers with
amputation and the cauſtic. It muſt be confeſſed,

I   however,

however, that his *language* is fufficiently fcientific. " Whilſt the diftempers of a *relaxed fibre prognoſti-* " *cate* and *prepare* all the *morbid force* of *convulſion* " in the body of the ſtate, the ſteadineſs of the " *phyſician* is over-powered," &c. " The *doctor* " of the conſtitution ſhrinks from his own *ope-* " *ration.* He doubts and queſtions the ſalutary " but critical terrors of the *cautery* and the *knife.*" The doctor thus difgraced, anon he becomes a foldier, learns the Brunſwick march, and " takes " a poor credit even from defeat." Then again he is an eulogiſt ; a politician ; a lawyer ; a re- furrection-man, dealing in rotten carcafes ; a " juriſt ;" a letter-founder, and a printer's devil ; an engroffer of parchment rolls, and an engraver of brazen tablets : and all in one ſingle page.

And now he is a dancing maſter, whimfically enough employed in " *bowing* to the enemy " abroad," which, it is fagacioufly remarked, is not the way " to fubdue the *conſpirator* *" who is breaking the fiddle " at home." Having dif- played thefe harlequin tricks in his own perfon, he proceeds to try his dagger of lath upon other objects. In ten little lines " anarchy" is a rattle- fnake ; a " *focus*," endowed with magnetic powers ; a " venomous and blighting infect," that

---

* *Conſpirator !* fingular number !—" A man may confpire with hImfelf ! ! !"—*Chief Juſtice* EYRE.—*State Trials*, King *v.* J. Thelwall, *fifth day.*

" blaſts

" blafts and fhrivels, and burns up the promife of
" the year," occafions " falutary and beautiful
" *inftitutions* to *yield duft and fmut*," and turns " the
" harveft of the law to ftubble." At laft, to
crown the whole, tired of agriculture and natural
hiftory, and having panted round the whole circle of metaphor, he returns, like a hare to the
fquat he ftarted from, takes up his old profef-
fion of phyfic again, and gives us an emetic of
puftles and blotches, and " eruptive difeafes,"
which " fink in and re-appear by fits." The ma-
lady, however, which is now under his care,
whatever it may be, has, fomehow or other, *a
converfable faculty*—a fort of *intellectual* " *fuel*,"
which holds treafonable correfpondence " with
" the fource of regicide," and cunningly " waits
" for the favourable moment of a freer commu-
" nication to exert and to encreafe its force."
This is really the moft intelligent, artful, intri-
guing, philofophifing difeafe I ever heard of.
What a lofs to the readers of " Medical Tranf-
" actions," that the doctor has not favoured us
with its name, its diagnofis, and the peculiar cha-
racteriftics of its exterior fymptoms.

Wonderful man ! moft incongruous, and moft
brilliant phenomenon of genius ! how haft thou
the power to make even nonfenfe fafcinating, and
give charms to fheer malevolence ! Thou art, indeed, a compound at once ftrange and terrible :

but,

but, it muſt be confeſſed, thou art an entertaining mongrel. Full of beauty, and of ferocity, as the *royal* beaſt of Bengal ; and driven onward by the fame blind impulſe of rage and ravin—thy hideous roar is ever prophetic of blood : But " the " tyger is frequently loſt in the ape ;" and indignation is diſarmed by ſplendid abſurdity :—while the tricks and antics of a wild, extravagant, frantic imagination have a ſort of witching charm, that defies the ſober ſeverity of judgment, and occaſions even the abſurdity itſelf, to be accepted as a ſort of atonement for the depravity we ſhould elſe abhor !

But let us not forget—for if we ſhould, there are others who will remember, that theſe tropes, and metaphors, and allegories, however wild and incoherent in themſelves, all point to one determinate objeet—all lead to one concluſion : namely, that the eighty thouſand jacobins (more or leſs) who are ſo firmly grounded in the truth and purity of their ſentiments, that no ſophiſtical " reaſoning," no hackney " argument" of prejudice or corruption, " no example" of government ſpies caught in their own vile nooze, " no " venerable authority ! can have the ſlighteſt in- " fluence upon them ;" and whoſe conduet is ſo ſtrictly conſonant with benevolence and juſtice, that when the crown (that is to ſay the miniſter)
brings

brings them before a jury, howſoever ſelected, and of whomſoever compoſed, it retires from its courts defeated and diſgraced—That theſe deteſtable jacobins—theſe eighty thouſand criminals, againſt whom no crime can be proved—theſe conſpirators, who never yet conſpired—theſe aſſaſſins, whoſe only dagger is reaſon, and whoſe only ſword is truth—the meridian ſun itſelf being their dark lanthorn, and publicity their only cloak—theſe are to be ſubmitted to the prompt execution of the cautery and the knife; to be cut and burnt away, like warts, from the eruptive body. All, all who dare to complain, though oppreſſion were heaped upon oppreſſion, " till it o'ertopp'd Olympus"—all, all who dare to wiſh for change, (though tyranny grew black as thickeſt night, and corruption ſtank in our very pottage,) all are to be ſwept away. Jurors (unleſs juries can be regulated by ſome new faſhion) muſt no more be truſted with ſuch conſpirators: for jurors are conſpirators themſelves —" the acquittal of the conſpirators is a proof " of the extent to which the conſpiracy had " ſpread *." Juries will not do: our preſent tribunals are not efficient. They were inſtituted

* Such was the audacious language of William Pitt. His mind ſeems pretty well diſpoſed for the adoption of *the cautery and the knife.* His *ſteadineſs* would not be much *overpowered by the operation.*

for

for the purpofe of chaftifing criminal ACTS—
they cannot reach OPINIONS with fufficient
certainty;—*but the* SWORD *can.* " Out the
" word came; and it never went back*:" nor
ever can get back. Mr. B. indeed foon repented
that he had let it out; and endeavoured to recal
it : but in vain. It had efcaped into the hands
of Mr. Owen; and by means of a fortunate
quarrel, between the apoftate politician and the
apoftate bookfeller, behold—we have it. It is
before the world. It is in print. " The type
" is black and legible;" and both " the *letter*,"
and the fpirit are " *clear.*"

" I have formerly heard," fays he †, *with more
furprife than* " *fatisfaction,*" that " opinions are
" things out of human jurifdiction,"—that " you
" can never extirpate opinion, without extir-
" pating a whole nation." He then proceeds
to argue both the practicability, and the propriety
of this forcible extirpation; maintaining the juftice of " war againft opinion ‡," and even affirm-
ing, in round terms, " when I am told it is a war
" of opinions, I am told it is the moft important
" of all wars §." He does not, however, neglect
the opportunity of expofing the inconfiftency
of his antagonifts. I am glad he does not. I

---

* Letters, p. 171.   † Thoughts p. 63.‡   Ibid. 64.
§ Thoughts, p. 66.

would

would not have the intemperance, or the injuſtice, of either party ſpared. All perſecution, from whatever quarter it come, (and I call all war upon opinion, all proſecution for opinion, perſecution) is equally deteſtable : nay, if the thing, in itſelf, is capable of aggravation, that aggravation it receives, when it is appealed to by the friends of liberty. Let prieſts and tyrants take ſhelter in their inquiſitions, their ſtar-chambers, and their courts of law, where their *blind* deity, with the two-edged ſword, uplifts her ſcales, in pageant mockery, but ſtrikes as power directs. We have a goddeſs of more perfect organ—far-ſeeing Reaſon, of ſteadier balance, and unweaponed hand ; but, yet, of force that cannot fail of victory, if we have faith, and truſt in her omnipotence.

Why ſhould any advocate for freedom have loſt his temper, or his conſiſtency, on account of any nonſenſe which Mr. Reeves might chooſe, or be hired, to write, about the trunk, or the branches of a rotten tree ? In the name of wonder, what can we wiſh for more, than that *ſuch talents* ſhould be employed in *ſuch a cauſe*. I, at leaſt, have never ſuſpected Mr. Reeves of being one, who, if the Thames were a fire, would know where to run for water to put out the flames. But if ever it ſhould pleaſe the gods to enable him to write any thing worth anſwering, let us hope that pen, ink, and paper will not be wanting. Write away then,

Juſtice

Juftice Reeves, and fupport your caufe. Scalp
headlefs wights with Grub-ftreet "Tomahawks;"
and indite new " Thoughts*" for men who never
think. I, meanwhile, proceed to examine the arguments of your more potent coadjutor.

" As to the *mere matter of extirpation*," fays he,
" of all kinds of opinions, *whether right or wrong*,
" without the extirpation of a people †"—O certainly : it is not neceffary to extirpate the *whole*
people : Cut but the throats of *that portion* of a
people who hold the obnoxious opinion—*Saint
Bartholomife* them—nay, that *informed, difcuffing* portion of them—that *awakened,* able, energetic band,
fuch as the profcribed eighty thoufand of this
country, over whom " No *example*" (however terrible) " *no venerable authority* can have the flight-
" eft influence"—*Do but Bartholomife them*, and
the bufinefs *appears* to be done. And this, fays the
Oracle of ariftocratical abhorrence of maffacre
and cruelty—" this is a thing fo very common,
" that would be clouded and obfcured, rather than
" illuftrated, by examples."

Mr. B. was very much in the right to fave himfelf from the confufion, in which particular ftatements would have involved him, by this round
and general affertion ; for certainly, if he had

* Thoughts on the Englifh Government.
† Thoughts on the Regicide Peace, p. 64.

come

come to clofe quarter with facts, none of the particular ftatements would have anfwered his purpofe: certainly the maffacre of the proteftants,
by the *humane* and *politic* old defpotifm of France,
would not: though for this our *ferious* Machiavel
(for the Italian did but jeft) could, perhaps, affign
a reafon. The thing was not thoroughly done.
It is true, that the *Grand Monarque* having determined to " exert a vigour beyond the law," and
having given orders accordingly*, " there were
" killed in the city of Paris, that day and the
" next, above ten thoufand, whereof above five
" hundred were barons, knights, and gentlemen,
" who were purpofely met together, from all parts,
" to honour the king of Navar's marriage."—It is
true, " Gafper de Coligny, the famous admiral,"
(one of the leaders of the Hugonots) " was pulled
" out of the ftable, and cruelly abufed by the fury
" of the common people," (this was a royalift mob
---a mob hired, inftigated, marfhalled by the *regular*,
conftituted government) " who detefting his very
" name, *tore* his head from his fhoulders, cut off
" his hands, and dragging him through the ftreets
" to the place of execution, left him hanging by

* See Englifh Tranflation of *Davila*, p. 374, 375, and
376, edit. 1647. See alfo for the horrible particulars, " Hif-
" tory of the bloody Maffacres, &c. in 1572" (extracted from
" Thuanus's Hift. of his own times," and tranflated.) Lond.
1674.

K   " one

" one of his feet upon the gallows ; and a few
" days after" (thefe were royalift cannibals!)" they
" fet fire to it upon the fame gallows, half burning
" it, with barbarous rejoicings ; their cruelty find-
" ing no end, till two fervants of the Marefhal de
" Momorancy ftole away the relics of his mifera-
" ble carcafe, and buried them, fecretly, at Chan-
" tilly." It is true, alfo, that " the day before
" this terrible execution, the king difpatched
" pofts into divers parts of the kingdom, com-
" manding the governors of cities and provinces
" to do the like."—It is true, that " on the fame
" night at Meaux, and the days enfuing at Or-
" leans, Rouën, Bourges, Angiers, Thouloufe,
" and many other places, but above all, at
" *Lyons*, there was a moft bloody flaughter of
" the Hugonots, *without any refpeƈt of age or fex*,
" or quality of perfons." But it is true, alfo, that
through the great extent, and out of the whole
population of France, there were *only* forty thoufand men, women, and children put to the fword.
There ought to have been eighty thoufand, reafoning, difcourfing, enquiring adults, even if the
population of France had only equalled that of
Britain. Hence, perhaps, it was, that *Hugonot
Jacobinifm* and *Hugonot infidelity* (or *Hugonot herefy*—
for with *eſtablifhed prieſts* they are *eſſentially* the
fame!) inftead of being " extirpated" from
" the vicinage of Europe," have been gaining
ground

ground ever fince, both in number of profelytes, and extent of principle.

Neither will " the wars of Charles V. and his " fucceffors," againft this fame *Hugonotifm*, better fupport his caufe ; as indeed he confeffes : though at the fame time he cautioufly obferves, that whether thofe wars " might or might not" be juftified, " is " a matter of hiftorical criticifm !" Nor yet will he be able to quote, among his " cloud of ex- " amples," the early perfecutions of the Chrif- tian fyftem of innovation and reform : a fyftem which, whatever Mr. B.'s *mode of faith* may fug- geft, went much greater lengths, with refpect to a very tender fubject, than the wildeft *Atheifm* either of the French or Englifh Jacobins. The primitive Chriftians (as every fcholar knows) both upheld and practifed, not only *equality of rights*, but *community of goods :* (a wild and abfurd fcheme, I confefs ; and not practicable upon any *large fcale :* but I fpeak to the doctrinal and hiftorical fact :) nor can the man who has ferioufly confider- ed the effential doctrines of that religion, view, without contempt, the oftentatious mockery of a modern corgregation, who call it Chriftianity to keep " the poor, the halt, and the blind," ftand- ing, at due diftance, in the aifles, while the well- dreffed claffes are clofeted up in pews, lined, elevated, and embellifhed, according to the rank and ftation of the occupants, liftening to a drawler

K 2   in

in an awkward habit, and cooped up in a maho-
gany box, to foothe the pride of greatnefs with
obfequious exhortations, and terrify the abjeft and
opprcffed into trembling fubordination, and reve-
rence for their *betters*. Edifices, thus *fet out*, are
Pagan theatres; not Chriftian churches. What
degree of perfecution this fyftem met with in
Pagan countries, is a fubjeft of fo much con-
troverfy among the learned, that I fhall not venture to decide. However, that it was perfecuted
in " that centre and focus of innovation," Judea,
where it firft broke out, is evident; and that with
tolerable feverity. It was perfecuted. Chrift became popular. His doftrines became popular.
—How could doftrines fail of popularity, which
contained fo many elementary political truths,
and vindicated, fo direftly, in many refpefts at
leaft, the Rights of Man ? He did not fpare corruptions, either in Church or State. He expofed
the doftrines and the praftices of the priefts and
the ariftocrats, the Pharifees and the Sadducees,
the powerful, the wealthy, and the great. He
collefted the people together, in great numbers,
and leftured them againft exifting abufes; in the
ftreets, in the wildernefs, in the fields, and on the
neighbouring hills. The government was alarm-
ed. They " fought to deftroy him;" and when
they could not " lay hold of his words," they fet
gangs of ruffians upon him, to knock him on the
head,

head, with bludgeons and ftones. But " he. " efcaped out of their hands, and got away." In the midft of thefe perfecutions, the number of his profelytes continually encreafed; and fome of the *great men* among the Jews (like the *great man* I had mentioned in the " Narrative of my arreft and treatment *") thought, " that men who " had a heap of people running after them, " were beft in a place of fecurity." He was fecured. A certain apoftate (his name was neither *Edmund Burke*, *William Pitt*, nor *William Windham* —it was *Judas Ifcariot*) took it into his head to perfecute the doctrines he had formerly fupported ; betrayed the caufe ; and accepted a penfion for " his public fervices." In fhort, Jefus Chrift wascrucified, as *Jofeph Gerrald* hasbeen tranfported, for expofing the corruption and degeneracy of the times, and preaching a great reform. But it was all in vain. Hang, tranfport, and crucify, as long as you pleafe : the fpirit of a great reformer, martyr'd for a glorious principle, will rife again. The phœnix mind fprings triumphant from the pyre; and the winds, that fcatter the afhes of the martyr, propagate the principles for which he fell.

Thus fared it with Chriftianity. The perfecutions it fuffered, by drawing attention to its doc-

* Tribune, vol. I. p. 89.

trines

trines (many of which, particularly in the ftate
of fociety then prevailing, were excellently calculated to imprefs the general mind) contributed,
more than all the tales of prophecies and miracles, with which it *became* incorporated, to fpread
the fyftem, not only through Judea, but through
" all the furrounding vicinage." *It did continue to
fpread fo long as perfecution continued* ; *and never was
overthrown till* POLITIC EMPERORS *(finding it a
ufeful inftrument of ambition)* ESTABLISHED THE
NAME, AND DESTROYED THE PRINCIPLE.

But, fays Mr. B. opinions may not only be
forced; you may even force men into the forcible perfecution of their own opinions:—" In-
" ftances enough may be furnifhed of people who
" have enthufiaftically, and with force, propa-
" gated thofe opinions, which, fome time before,
" they refifted with their blood *." True: but it
is a truth which makes terribly againft *one* part
of his argument, and nothing for the other—for
it tends to fhew (if brought to the teft of facts)
the great advantages which new opinions have
over the old, when driven to the iffue of coercion. The profelytizing army is always encreaf-
ing; the army of eftablifhments always falling
away. Many thoufands, in every long-continued
ftruggle, begin with " refifting opinions with their

---

* Thoughts, p. 64.

" blood,"

" blood," on account of their *novelty*, which they
conclude with " propagating (even enthufiafti-
" cally, and with force,") from a conviction of
their *truth*. An Arnold, or a Dumourier, may be
dragged from the retreats of infamy, to prove that
the Champions of Liberty may be bought by its
foes. But the examples are worth but little, in
the fcale of argument; and, I fpeak it with
glowing fatisfaction, they are but few. As for
the voluntary, and unbought recantations, they
are all on the other fide. In fhort, " in the event
" of a ftruggle," fettled governments may reft
almoft affured, that they muft conquer immediately, or not at all. It is, therefore, a ferious
thing, to bring matters to fuch an iffue.

I rather fuppofe, however, that Mr. B. had his
eye upon examples of another kind ; for fpeci-
mens of which, not to burthen the reader with
quotations, efpecially, as I have cited the paffage
in a former publication * ; I refer to " Burnet's
" Summary of Affairs before the Reftoration †."
There he will find *Lutherans*, *Catholics*, and *Cal-
vinifts*—that is to fay, Lutheran, Catholic, and
Calvinift *Princes*—Electors, Dukes, and Palatines,
in abundance, changing, and re-changing their
religion, as policy of ftate directed ; and propagating, with *force*, at one time, " thofe opinions

* Pol. Lect. p. 55. *On Prof. for Pol. Opinion.*
† Own Times, vol. I. p. 14. fol. edit.

" which,

" which, before, they refifted with *their* blood :"
—that is to fay, with the blood which they regarded as *their property*—the blood of their fub-
jeɛts : the faɛt being, that, like princes and ftatef-
men in general, they had no fettled opinion of
any kind ; except, that whatever tended to gra-
tify their ufurping ambition, was to be purfued;
and that every thing was to be " judged by moral
" prudence " (of which they were fole umpires)
" and not by any abftraɛt principle of right * ."

But, continues the advocate of extirpation—
" Rarely *have ever* great changes in opinion taken
" place, without the application of force, more
" or lefs†." True, Mr. B.—and for this plain reafon—governments have rarely wanted fuch coun-
fellors as yourfelf, to perfuade them to drive the
queftion to that iffue. Eftablifhments (however
pure in the outfet) have never failed, in procefs of
time, to be infeɛted with innumerable corruptions. Thefe the governors have an intereft in per-
petuating ; and, indeed, for the fake of that intereft, the corruptions have been generally intro-
duced. To them, " the beauty of all Conftitu-
" tions confifts in thofe very corruptions of which
" others complain ‡;" for it is by the latter, not

---

* Thoughts, p. 64.　　　† Ibid. p. 65.
‡ Speeches of the Right Hon. W. Pitt, and Lord Morning-
ton, on the Motion for a Committee to take into confideration
the Petition of the Friends of the People.

the

the former, that their ambition is flattered, their rapacity indulged, their patronage extended, and places and penfions heaped upon themfelves, their families, and dependants. Thefe corruptions are therefore artfully confounded, and incorporated, with the original inftitutions; and the inftitutions themfelves, under one pretence or other, are artfully abrogated by their pretended fupporters; till, at laft, the whole is infected; and nothing but corruption remains. The enormity of the evil produces complaint. Remonftrance, rejected and defpifed, provokes to keener difcuffion, and more bold enquiry. New theories and new fyftems are ftarted, more confonant with the nature of man, and principles of juftice; and the old, corrupted, disjointed, patch-works of obfolete inftitution, and new-fangled ufurpation, are attacked with all the ftrength of argument, and the ardour of principled conviction. But corruption cannot ftand the teft of enquiry. It fhrinks from the galling probe of truth. Its ftrength confifts in " the morbid force of convulfion," not in the confcious energies of temperate health. It therefore flies from argument, and appeals to force: leaving, to the profcribed reformers, only the fad alternative of perifhing in thoufands, according to the example of the Hugonots, and the advice of Burke and Windham, by " a vigour beyond the " law," or of repelling force by force, with

L   death

death or victory on their banners, and on their hearts.

Such has been the cafe in many a nation—in Genoa—in Switzerland—in Holland *twice*—in America; and fuch was the cafe in France. Opinion had grown till it had burft its chains; circumftances concurred that gave opinion weight: the court feemed to yield; but coercion was prepared. Monopolies (gigantic in wickednefs) were planned and executed, to put the fubfift-,ence of the people in the power of their op-preffors; and frefh maffacres were refolved, and organifed: but the project tranfpired: force was repelled by force: *Lambefque* was difcomfited; the people flew to arms; the Baftille was taken; *Broglio* fled; and Paris efcaped a fecond feaft of Saint Bartholomew. But ftill there were *filver-headed* traitors to the caufe of man, penfioned profligates, at the ear of royalty, advifing coercion —from within, or from without—it mattered not. A foreign combination produced a foreign war; and Louis XVI, who had fworn to defend the *conftitution of new opinions*, kept up (as *Mallet du Pan*, his confidential agent confeffes, in his *Cor-refpondance Politique pour Servir a l'Hiftoir)* a fecret intercourfe with the defpots who had leagued for its deftruction. But furely the " great changes " in opinion," refulting from " the application
" of

" of force," in thefe inftances, are not much cal‑
culated to encourage eftablifhed governments to
a repetition of the experiment.

I do not mean to affert, that coercion has no
influence over opinion. I have not forgotten that
the defpotifms of China, and Japan (defpotifms
in which that prompt conductor and diffeminator
of intellect, the prefs, is yet unknown*) did, by
nipping Chriftianity in the very bud (long before
it was eighty thoufand—perhaps before it was
eight hundred ftrong) exterminate that religion :
or, more properly, prevent it from taking root.
Neither do I forget the prophet of Mecca and his
armed apoftles ; who carried conviction on the
fabre's edge, propounding circumcifion or death.
But Mahomet, and his Arabs, alfo, war againft
Mr. B. : for here *the new opinion prevailed.* And
why did the new opinion prevail ? The anfwer is
a dreadful warning to old eftablifhments not to be
eager for contefts of blood. The new opinion
prevailed, becaufe there is an incalculable dif‑
tance between the energy and enthufiafm of a
new conviction, and the fcience and mechanifm
of ancient habits : becaufe it is the former, alone,
that roufes the full force of intellect and valour,

---

* The Chinefe have an art of printing. But it confifts
in the ufe of logographic characters, inftead of an alphabet :
it is, accordingly, a labour of many years to learn to read
their language.

and

and " fuffers not a particle of the man to be
" loft :" becaufe the old opinion depends upon
rotine; the new .upon intrepidity and merit:
becaufe in one, the mafs feel that they are nothing; in the other, they may be every thing
they dare : becaufe the eftablifhment takes its
leaders, and muft take them, by a *fort of lottery*,
from the court cabal; the innovation *felects* them
" from the ranks." In one cafe commands are
conferred, that laurels may be reaped: in the
other, laurels are reaped that commands may be
obtained. Such, ".in the event of a ftruggle,"
are the advantages in favour of the innovating
army: and Mr. B. fees, and has acknowledged
them in all their ftrength.

Yet, ftill this champion of old fyftems maintains, that new opinions may be, and ought to
be extirpated by force. They ought to be extirpated for three reafons. 1. Becaufe " *Opinion*
" *is the rudder of human action* *." Granted.
Granted, alfo, that " *as the opinion is wife or foolifh,*
" *vicious or moral, the caufe of action is noxious or fa-*
" *lutary.*" But who is to judge of this wifdom or
this folly—of this vice or this morality ? *Govern-*
ment ! fays Mr. B. I fay no : for that thing called
government, if there be corruption in the ftate, is,
of neceffity, the focus of that corruption : That
thing called government, is compofed of a privi-

* Thoughts, p. 65.

leged

leged few, who always may have; and, the hiftory of the world affures us, frequently have had,
an intereft diametrically oppofite to that of the
ftate. Was the court of Tarquin, of Nero, of
Caligula, Domitian, or Hiliagabalus, fit to be
confulted for ftandards of moral and intellectual
tafte? Did they not mow down all virtue and all
wifdom, and propagate the moft deteftable vices,
and the moft atrocious barbarifm? Are the governments of Japan, of Morocco, of Algiers, fit
to be confulted as oracles upon thefe fubjects?
If they are not, none are: and for this reafon, If
the government were ten times blacker than all
that I have inftanced, it would fay that it was
pure ; and the fouler it was, the more dangerous
to deny the dictum.

How then is it to be decided? *By precedent!*
you fay—No; for precedent is infinitely diverfi-
fied. All things may be fupported by precedent ;
and all condemned. It would, therefore, revert
to governments to decide what precedents were
good, and what were bad ; and all my former
objections recur——*By antiquity and eftablifhed ufage!*
No; that would be to profcribe all improvement
—for all improvement is change of eftablifhed
ufage. That would be to make the weaknefs
and fimplicity of childhood a ftandard for the vigour and intelligence of maturity ; and to prohi-
bit all the advantages of experience. As Lord
Bacon

Bacon obferves, in this refpect, *we, who live now, are, in reality, the ancients ; they are the younger gene-rations that have paffed before.*

Every thing ufeful to man has refulted from this great principle. Every improvement, every in-vention, is an innovation, refting upon the fub-ftantial data—that, by having all the experience of our anceftors, with the addition of our own, we are wifer than they ; and have a right, not only to imitate, like apes, but to improve—to alter—to choofe, and to change, as men.

And is political fcience, alone, upon whofe im-provement depend the happinefs, and the lives of millions, and the creation, as it were, of new worlds of population, whofe embryons are now perifhing in the dark and comfortlefs chaos of de-vouring defpotifm—Is political fcience alone to be an exception to the rule, and never to be breeched in manhood, becaufe it has formerly been encumbered with fwathing-bands and long coats ? Certainly ; and, for this obvious reafon, that the nurfes, who hold the leading ftrings, have a profit in its weaknefs ; and muft lofe their places, and their perquifites, by fuch a change. The cafe of governments, and of arts and fciences, in this refpect, are faid to be effentially different ; but the difference confifts in this alone : and if we had a government of tanners, and a priefthood of fawyers, I have no doubt that it would be high treafon

treafon to drefs a hide after a new fafhion, and blafphemy to invent machines for fplitting timber.

2. " *It has ever been the great, primary objeſt of ſpeculative and doſtrinal philoſophy, to regulate opinion.*" Certainly, and this objeſt has always been, and of neceffity muft be, moft effectually anfwered when opinion is moft free ; as indeed the very terms, " fpeculative and doſtrinal " philofophy," when ufed in any fenfe of approbation, take for granted. Every body knows that *philoſophy* means the *love of wiſdom* ; and that to *ſpeculate* is to *conjeſture, and pry, and enquire,* *with a view to the diſcovery of truths as yet unknown.* So that fpeculative philofophy evidently means *the love of that wiſdom which conſiſts in making enquiries and conjeſtures, with a view to the diſcovery of new truths* ; while *doſtrinal* philofophy, or the philofophy of *teaching,* muft of neceffity mean *that love of wiſdom which diſplays itſelf in imparting to mankind the truths which, in the proceſs of our conjeſtures and enquiries we may have diſcovered.* Now how can we fpeculate without the liberty of fpeculation ? How can truths, hitherto unknown, be difcovered, if we are not at liberty to conjeſture and enquire ?—And how can new truths be taught, if the philofopher is not at liberty to communicate what his conjeſtures and enquiries have led him to regard as true ? In fhort, how can

there

there be any fuch thing as " fpeculative and doc-
" trinal philofophy," if opinion is not left un-
fhackled? It is not by coercion, but by difcuffion,
that opinion is to be regulated, and the defirable
effects of morality and good conduct are to be obtained. But,

3. " *It is the great object of political philofophy to
promote that* [*opinion*] *which is found.*" Certainly, it
is the duty of the political philofopher, and of
every philofopher, by every motive of reafon, and
every opportunity of difcuffion, to promote whatever appears to him to be found. But the difpo-
fition to decide between foundnefs and unfound-
nefs by the faggot and the axe, comes not from
the fchools of philofophy, but from thofe of theological contention. What follows, therefore,
" *and to* EXTIRPATE *what is mifchievous, and*
" *which directly tends to render men bad* CITIZENS
" *in the community, and mifchievous neighbours out of*
" *it,*" is a fophifm both in terms and fubftance. It
is a fophifm in fubftance, in as much as the ftatement being general, vague, and hypothetical, fur-
nifhes no juft foundation for the particular conclufion meant to be inferred. It is a fophifm in terms,
in as much as the phrafe, " extirpating what is
" mifchievous," being fpoken in reference to the
antecedent " political philofophy," demands affent
only to the propriety of extirpating the fuppofed
mifchievous opinion by philofophical means—
that

that is to fay, by means of reafon, or fetting one opinion againft another; while the whole tenor of the argument would apply this affent, not to extirpation by philofophy, but by the fword. —In this fenfe of the word, therefore, I deny the propofition : a propofition, indeed, which abfolutely begs the queftion ; and affirms the very point it pretends to argue. I, on the other hand, affirm, that political philofophy has no right (according to Mr. B.'s jargon) to extirpate, by force, any opinion whatever :—no, not even " the opi" nion, that it is a man's duty to take from me " my goods, and to kill me if I refift him." The fophift who fhould propound fuch a doctrine, would be eafily confuted. [To fay, that he could not, is to admit that he is right ; or to affirm, that falfehood is more convincing than truth: a dictum that deftroys all morals.] He who fhould *act* upon the doctrine, would, undoubtedly, be hanged. But fo long as indolence, or fear, reftrains him from action, *the opinion*, however abfurd, is perfectly harmlefs ; and fociety ought to be fatisfied. It is fufficient for the *law*, that we fear the *gallows :* Our friends and companions, it is true, the guardians of our interefts, and the inftructors of our children, we would feek among men who act upon more generous principles.

As for pulling down governments—in addition to the preceding arguments, I fhall only add, that *no man* can pull down a government. But when,

M   not

not a Man, but a *People*, wills a grand renovation, to feel the *will* is alfo to be confcious of the power : and, when the will and the power co-operate, fophifts may ftring fyllogifms, like beads upon a rofiary ; but while they are reafoning, the thing is done.

Fortunately for mankind, this will is not lightly infpired. It is not to be produced by declamations or logic. The fpeculative few will have their preferences, their theories, and their projeﬅed improvements. Sir Thomas Moore had his Eutopia ; and Hume, himfelf, fketched a fort of ground-plot for the French Republic : but to the mafs, even of thofe who have fome " tolerable " leifure for difcuffion, and fome means of infor- " mation," (fo long as their grievances are not very galling) that which *is* will generally appear to be beft, merely becaufe it *is* ; and becaufe that fpirit of nationality, which belongs to the whole fpecies, occafions us to imbibe, with our very nutriment, a prejudice in favour of our national inftitutions. Nay, even the fpeculative few, themfelves, from their very love of fpeculation, till roufed by fome extraordinary provocative, prefer the very eftablifhments they difapprove, to the dangers, and the trouble of a change.—Hume's Commonwealth flept for fixty years, and the Eutopia for whole centuries, on the fhelves of the learned ; and even the popular language

of

of Thomas Paine would not have provoked any
very alarming difcuffion, if the general *condition* of
mankind had not pre-difpofed them to exclaim—
We are wretched!—*Let us enquire the caufe!*

In fhort, in all the pages of hiftory I have pe-
rufed, there is not a fingle inftance (and moft affuredly I have not forgotten France) of a great,
popular revolution taking place, till grinding, and
long-continued oppreffion, had rendered it abfolutely neceffary :—till groaning Nature called for
the dire relief.

It is not, therefore, by the extermination of
eighty thoufand mal-contents and theoretical reformers, but by the alleviation of burthens, and
the reftoration of equal juftice, that fuch revolutions are to be avoided. It is not by the perfecution of *new opinions*, but by the reform of *old
abufes*, that contentment can be reftored, and tranquillity preferved to a ftate ; and governors fecured from the terrors of retributive juftice.

But, fays Mr. B. I do not mean to perfecute all
new doctrines. " Theological opinions," for example, " whether found or erroneous, do not go
" directly to the well-being of focial, of civil, or
" of politic fociety." [If I were difpofed to give
a clue to one fort of perfecution, while I repro-
bate another, I could mention fome theological
opinions which appear to me, at leaft, to go more
directly to the deftruction of all focial, moral, and

political

political virtue, than any thing of which Atheifin
itfelf was ever accufed. " If I were the Deity,"
fays Plutarch, who, by the way, was himfelf a
prieft—but he was, alfo, a philofopher—a moral
philofopher !—" If I were the Deity, I would ra-
" ther that men fhould deny my exiftence,
" than fay, that I was cruel, jealous, lafcivious,
" or revengeful*."] The theological dogmatifts,
he continues, " did not preach vices or crimes."
[How, Mr. B.—did they not preach the crufade?
Did they not preach murder, affaffination, poifon-
ing, *depofition of Kings*, the axe, the halter, and the
faggot ? And did they not practife what they
preached ?—But I forget myfelf—With the fingle
exception of *depofing kings*, all that I have objected,
inftead of vices and crimes, are virtues, in Mr. B.'s
politico-moral code. Nay, even fuch depofition itfelf,
provided the power be transferred only to the
privileged bodies, and feudal proprietories of the
" old Germanic or Gothic cuftumary," may be
perfectly innocent, and even praife-worthy : for
" indeed, the force and form of the inftitution,
" called States, continued, in *greater perfection*, in
" thofe republican communities (in which the
" claffes, orders, and diftinctions, fuch as before
" fubfifted, or nearly fuch, were ftill left) than un-
" der monarchies †."] " The parties," fays he (the

* I quote from memory : but I know, that in fentiment, I
am correct.   † Letters, p. 111.

religionifts)

religionifts) " difputed on the beft means of pro-
" moting virtue, religion, and morals." And
what do the Atheift and the Chriftian difpute
about?—Why, whether religion is, or is not, the
beft inftrument for promoting morals and virtue*.
Men may differ upon this point, as well as upon
the queftion, of which fort of religion (from the
Egyptian faith, in calves and onions, to the or-
thodox metaphyfician's, in an incomprehenfible,
immaterial, triune Deity) and yet both parties may
be good members of fociety. Do you try our
lives by our opinions, or our opinions by our
lives? Neither would be juft: for man is an incongruous animal. But furely, the latter were
the more candid: and, upon this foundation, I
would be bound to bring Atheifts into court, before
whom the pious, impetuous, hireling apoftate of
Beaconsfield muft hide his head in confufion.

Opinions certainly have their tendencies with
refpect to moral character. But opinions are
multitudinous. They proceed not from any
one common ftock. They fpring up from many a
wildly fcattered feed. They bloffom on innumerable ftems. Detefted, therefore, be the bigotry that
condemns the whole foil, on account of one rank
weed: that, from a particular doctrine, however
erroneous, would argue the immorality of a general character!

* They difpute, alfo, whether religion be true or falfe. But
with this abftraction. the politician has nothing to do.

But

But " is there no diſtinction between an in-
" nocent and moral liberty," and opinions that
are " the direct highway to every crime and
" every vice ?"—Muſt government " either throw
" the bridle on the neck of headlong nature, or
" tie it up for ever to the poſt * ?" The ſophiſm
is ſtated with moſt plauſible ſubtilety; and the
ſimile is truely faſcinating: and when mankind
ſhall acknowledge themſelves to be horſes—or
that their governments are created for the expreſs
purpoſe of riding them, then will it ſtrictly apply:
then will it be right, that opinion ſhould be
laſhed round the ſtation-poſt, till it is broken-in
to the taſte of the rider. But ſo long as men
and their governors are animals of the ſame
order—ſo long as the great body of the people
have a *common weal*, and that little corporation
called Government, a *particular* one—ſo long as
rulers have an intereſt, and betray an inclination,
to conſider every thing as " an innocent and
" moral liberty," which tends to pamper their
ambition and rapacity, or encreaſe their power;
and to repreſent all opinion inconſiſtent with
their views, and hoſtile to their corrupt and deſ-
potic pride, as " the down-hill way to every crime
" and every vice"—ſo long (that is to ſay, as
long as political ſociety exiſts) will it be much
more dangerous to the peace and welfare of the
univerſe, to give the reins to that dread War-Horſe,

* Thoughts p. 66.

Conſtituted

Conftituted Power—*whofe neck is clothed with thunder, the glory of whofe noftrils is terrible, and who fwalloweth the ground with fiercenefs and rage,* than to throw them loofe on the neck of the headlong colt Opinion, who, though he may fnort, and curvet, and frolic through a thoufand extravagancies, will never, unlefs cruelly lafhed and goaded, commit any ferious depredations, or do irreparable mifchief, either to himfelf or others.

This metaphor is, however, an important part of Mr. Burke's ftatement; inafmuch, as it proves, that his obfervations on the forcible extirpation of opinion, are intended to apply, not only to the foreign war, but, alfo, to the *Domeftic Enemy.* Here, then, the argument, as far as relates to the dévelopement of the mind and obje&t of the writer, is complete—And thus it ftands :

There are, in this country, " eighty thoufand " Jacobins, utterly incapable of amendment, over " whom no argument, no example, no vene- " rable authority, can have the flighteft influ- " ence."

Thefe Jacobins have been tried, in the perfons of their fuppofed leaders; but " the tribunals " have been found inefficient ;" the Juries, (by finding them " Not Guilty") have " difowned the " government ;" and " public profecutions have " become mere fchools of treafon."

But

But opinions, if they cannot otherwife be checked, ought to be " extirpated by force :" the practicability of which may be proved " by a " cloud of examples."

Ergo—Eighty thoufand Jacobins are to be *forcibly* got rid of, at any rate ; " by the cauftic " and the knife ;" by fire and fword—by mock trial, without Juries to " difown the govern- " ment,"—or by the murderous tumults of Lynn and Yarmouth bludgeon-men.

Such, my fellow-citizens! are the propofitions and denunciations of the confidential hireling of a court, which yet fills the world with fenfelefs howlings againft cannibal philofophy, and affected exaggerations of revolutionary maffacres!!! And to fhew you that the infinuations of Mr. B. are not rafhly, or unadvifedly made—to fhew you the object of his infinuations—and that thefe hints do actually, and *bona fide*, come from the governing powers, for the purpofe of preparing the public mind for fome frefh member of " that *previoufly di-* " *gefted plan, or feries of meafures,*" hinted at in the memorable debates of the laft feffion ; effential parts of the language of thefe pamphlets—important branches of this *fyllogifm of maffacre*, are inceffantly propounded by all the members and dependants of the government ; no opportunity is neglected of infulting and reprobating the Juries who were guilty of the *deplored* acquittal ; the circumftance

circumſtance is openly connected with every motion and propoſition for encreaſing the military
force ; and Mr. Pitt (even ſince theſe ſheets have
been at the preſs) in a debate (*Oct.* 31.) upon that
very ſubject, affirms, that, notwithſtanding the
iſſue of the trials, nine-tenths of the nation are
convinced of our guilt. The inference is plain.
It is a commentary (a tremendous commentary,
coming from ſuch a quarter) on the intricate, yet
not obſcure text of the arch-apoſtate to Ariſto-
cratic moderation ! The ordinary phyſic of the
ſtate cannot cure the diſeaſe ; even extraordinary
potions have been adminiſtered without effect ;
and as ſoon as the body politic (that is to ſay,
the body of " political citizens,"—the privileged
" four hundred thouſand,") can be properly prepared for the operation, recourſe muſt be had to
" the cautery and the knife."

If this is not ſufficient to open your eyes, the
laſt trumpet alone can awaken you. If this is not
ſufficient to rouſe you to freſh vigilance, freſh
exertion, cloſer intercourſe, and intrepid unanimity, ye are dead—ye are loſt, not only " in the
" oblivious pool," but

> " In bottomleſs perdition ; there to dwell
> " In adamantine chains."

Think, I conjure you: What is the proſpect
held out to you ?—For yourſelves—unqualified

ſubmiſſion,

fubmiffion, or the prompt and deftroying vengeance of fome new mode of legalized maffacre,
or military execution :—for your children—the
tombftones of progenitors, who, though born to
a degree of freedom, which they were bound to
improve, and had no right to alienate, yet relin-
quifhed the patrimony, with criminal fupinenefs,
and left to them, for their inheritance, beggary,
and accumulating chains!

Roufe, then, once more, to the inveftigation of
your rights: for, if ye will be ignorant, ye muft
be flaves. Truft not your hopes to a blind fata-
lity. Repofe not in the indolent expectation,
that the corruption of the fyftem will work its
own cure. That corruption will, I believe, inevitably deftroy itfelf: But the deftruction of the
tyranny is not, of necellity, the emancipation of
the flave. Almoft all are tyrants when they have
the power: and the being, or the nation, that
knows not how to maintain its freedom, when
one yoke is broken, will find that another is
prepared. Even if a continuation of the war,
or the *winding-up* of a peace, fhould bring affairs
to a crifis—If, as is not unlikely, ere the clofe of
this century of ambition, ufurpation, and carnage,
prodigal expenditure fhould come to open bank-
ruptcy, and the obftinate infatuation of courtly
pride, fhould bring, at once, to their cataftrophe,

a fyftem

a fyftem of horrors and a miniftry of crimes;
how fhall ye be affured of benefitting by the
event?—How fhall ye fecure yourfelves from new
modes of corruption, and new fyftems of oppreffion? How, but by vigilent difcuffion, and well-
grounded principles?

Awake, then, once more, to the important
enquiry. Compare what ye are with what ye
have a right to be. Compare your powers
and your faculties with your condition: the
bounty of nature with your fcanty enjoyments,
and unfatisfied wants: the wealth refulting
from your productive labour, and the abject
wretchednefs of your general ftate. Compare
thefe things, and confider well the caufes. Trace
them to their fources, in the nature of fome,
and the corruptions of other, of thofe very inftitutions of the old Germanic, or Gothic cuftumary,
at the profpect of whofe approaching overthrow,
the volcanic imagination of Burke pours out fuch
deluges of flame and fmoke. Contraft the gloomy
intricacy of thefe oppreffive fyftems—thefe antique temples of fraud and violence, with the
fimple plans of reafon, and of nature; and learn
what to avoid, and what to purfue.

In the furtherance of this great enquiry, de-
fpife not the warnings, nor reject the affiftance
of a friend, whofe fincerity, at leaft, has been,
more than once, tried in the balance, and has not

been

been wanting; and who ftill, unfubdued by perfecutions, unawed by the daggers of affaffins, un-
chilled by the cold negleƈt of an unfocial world,
and forgetful of his own misfortunes, and his
own perfonal cares, incorporates himfelf with
the public, a ʒd with the warm enthufiafm of con-
viƈtion, proceeds to advocate the caufe of man
againft the ufurpations of eftablifhments.

Among the vindicators of thefe abufes, the
moft formidable, affuredly, is Edmund Burke:—
nay, he is the only one who, in any literary
point of view, can be regarded as formidable at all: for the talents of this country are,
generally fpeaking, pure : they have not been de-
bauched by court favour, nor rendered dependant.
by the liberal patronage of an adminiftration of
Mecænafes and Medici. In brilliancy of imagination, extent of general knowlege, and richnefs
and verfatility of talents, Mr. B. is, however, by
himfelf a hoft : though, at the fame time, fuch a
hoft as no champion of reafon, of an induƈtive
mind, and an enthufiaftic impreffion of truth,
need be afraid to attack. . Armed with thefe advantages, and thefe alone, I appear once more in
the lift ; and, not confcious of any difgrace in
a former fkirmifh, proceed to clofer and more decided confliƈt. He has ftated what he calls his
principles : mine fhall be ftated ftill more expli-
citly. I fhall demonftrate the mifery produced
by

by his feudal inftitutions ; and fhall endeavour to difplay the focial and moral advantages, the im-proved felicity and extended intelleft, which would refult from the more fimple and equitable fyftems dictated by the laws, and by the rights of nature.

In the pamphlet, or rather pamphlets, I am re-plying to, there are three important objefts of difcuffion. 1. The fpirit of Jacobinifm, in this country ; and the manner in which it ought to be difpofed of, or extirpated. 2.ᵉ The excellency of the old eftablifhed fyftems of government, as now adminiftered, and the folly, wickednefs, and profligacy of attempting to fhake them, either by fudden or progreffive change. 3. The juftice and propriety of the prefent war ; the capability of this country to purfue it, till what is affectedly ftyled regicide and atheifm, by eftablifhment, fhall be utterly deftroyed ; and the virtue, the wif-dom, and even the neceffity of ftaking our na-tional exiftence upon that iffue.

Of thefe, the firft only (which, though artfully incorporated with the reft, forms, in reality, a diftinft fubjeft) is particularly examined, in this letter ; to which I have given entirely a contro-verfial form ; as the nature of Mr. B's. attack, in reality, neceffitated me to do. The other two be-long to the comparifon of the refpeftive fyftems.

I fhall,

I fhall, therefore, in the following letters, proceed
to a fort of fyftematical developement of the
rights of nature, and genuine objects of focial inftitution ; and fhall, of courfe, controvert the axi-
oms and declamations of the arch-champion of
feudal barbarifm (which he calls polifhed fociety) as they fall in with the refpective heads :
and fhall thus endeavour to prefent, in living
colours, the contracted pictures of the ufurping eftablifhments, which court fycophants would have
you worfhip, and thofe natural and inalienable
rights, againft which they entertain fuch inveterate
abhorrence.

END OF LETTER I.

ADVERTISEMENT.

THERE is a clafs of Readers to whom it may, perhaps, appear neceffary to apologize for fomewhat of a different temper exhibited towards Mr. B. in the prefent pamphlet, from that which has been admitted, on all hands, to have diftinguifhed my Anfwer to his former Letter. But the apology muft be fought in the publications of my antagonift himfelf. If I have become more warm, it is becaufe the fentiments of Mr. B. have become more atrocious. His former attack was upon individuals: this is an outrage upon human nature: and he who can feek excufes to palliate the enormous profligacy of a wretch, who would extirpate opinions by the fword, and devote eighty thoufand of his fellow-citizens to judicial, or military maffacre, muft be deficient in that ardent benevolence, which, while it pants for the happinefs of man, cannot but deteft the fanguinary ferocity that yelps for wholefale carnage. Some, however, may think, that I am not without a fenfe of perfonal intereft, to ftir me, on this occafion. Perhaps it may be fo: But I am not, at the fame time, without my confolations. If the government fhould act upon the advice of Mr. B. my eyes will not be curfed with the fight of thofe horrors that muft inevitably enfue: Mine will be the glory, and the comparative felicity, of being one of the firft victims.

Beaufort Buildings, 5 *Nov.* 1796.